M000236120

WITHDRAWN
Jefferson County
Public Library-CO

Mother Tongue

A Saga of Three Generations of Balkan Women

What People Are Saying . . .

"Mother Tongue is a story about identity in the context of history. Romanov was born in just one place but the country she came from keeps changing as the tides of history keep sweeping over the Balkans. Framed as a journey to her family's hometown in what is now Croatia, Romanov's story is really about tracking the improbable line that led to who she is, down through her own life, her parents' lives and the lives of her ancestors. The Balkans are a tangle many of us tend to gloss over because we can't get inside it. With this fascinating memoir, Tania Romanov takes us there." —**Tamim Ansary, author of** *West of Kabul, East of New York*

"In Mother Tongue, a story for our times, writer, photographer and world traveler Tania Romanov follows the life journeys of three generations of women (Katarina, Zora and herself) as she pieces together a complex picture of the fragmentation, war and upheaval that has tormented the people of the area known as 'the Balkans' for centuries. As she digs deeper, painful truths are revealed, truths that lead her back to the refugee camp of her infancy and the losses and collateral damage of war." —**Linda Watanabe McFerrin, author of** *Namako, The Hand of Buddha* **and** *Dead Love*

"This is of historical and cultural significance. In a way, Romanov has done a service to every emigrant, to all the displaced persons out there, to the current refugee crisis, and done it by affirming the great value of "a melting pot." The forces that shape a people, that shape an individual person are so complex, and so easy to misunderstand — even by those they affect most deeply." **— Gay Wind Campbell, photographer, All Hands Volunteers, and author of** *Images Par Deux*

"I loved reading *Mother Tongue*. I absolutely devoured it, often reading in the middle of the night. I was always anxious to discover the next turn in the story and everyone's lives. I was totally engaged and every time I started asking myself a question, it was answered a few pages later. I really enjoyed the way the chronology came together, coming full circle at the end, with so much depth created throughout by the interwoven stories. I enjoyed not only learning more about Tania Romanov's family, but also gaining more insight into the complex political circumstances of these countries/peoples through time." **— Barbara Lannin, world traveler and business executive**

"I devoured Tania Romanov's *Mother Tongue* and wish I had read it before going to Croatia. I was drawn deeply into the turbulence of their lives along with the triumphs of overcoming obstacles, being reunited and finally flourishing. It made me a bit jealous of the strong ethnic identity and family bonds which I missed out on in my life. I will definitely return to the Adriatic coast, Croatia and more. Lots of memories flooded back as I read this book, although at the time I understood little of the lives of the people I encountered there, of the politics, or the history."
—**Susan Cornelis, author of *Conversations with the Muse: The Art Journal as Inner Guide***

"*Mother Tongue* is a book that successfully combines entertainment and education. Ms. Romanov tells the saga of her mother's family beautifully and with passion. I love the way she uses languages as an underlying theme of the book, tying the story lines together with the language she spoke only with her mother. It is a compelling tale full of interesting historical fact based on the author's research and her own knowledge and experiences."—**Judith Hamilton, author of *Animal Expressions***

Mother Tongue

A Saga of Three Generations of Balkan Women

TANIA ROMANOV

Travelers' Tales
An imprint of Solas House, Inc.
Palo Alto

Copyright 2018 by Tania Romanov Amochaev

All rights reserved. No part of this publication may be reproduced, distributed or transmitted in any form or by any means, including photocopying, recording, or other electronic or mechanical methods, without the prior written permission of the publisher, except in the case of brief quotations embodied in critical reviews and certain other noncommercial uses permitted by copyright law.

Travelers' Tales and Solas House are trademarks of Solas House, Inc., Palo Alto, California.

Travelerstales.com | solashouse.com

Cover design and interior layout by Ruth Schwartz,
aka My Book Midwife, mybookmidwife, com
based on a template © BookDesignTemplates.com

Cover photo: Katarina Marinovič's seven daughters,
including Zora Amochaev

Library of Congress Cataloging-in-Publication Data
Names: Amochaev, Tania Romanov, 1949- author.
Title: Mother tongue : a saga of three generations of Balkan women / Tania
 Romanov.
Description: 1st ed. | Palo Alto : Travelers' Tales, An imprint of Solas
 House, Inc., 2018.
Identifiers: LCCN 2017057379 (print) | LCCN 2017044333 (ebook) | ISBN
 9781609521523 | ISBN 9781609521288 (ebook)
Subjects: LCSH: Amochaev, Tania Romanov, 1949- | Amochaev, Tania Romanov,
 1949---Family. | Mothers and daughters--Yugoslavia--Biography. | Mothers
 and daughters--California--San Francisco--Biography. |
 Immigrants--California--San Francisco--Biography. |
 Refugees--Yugoslavia--Biography. | Yugoslavia--Emigration and immigration.
 | Yugoslavia--Biography. | San Francisco (Calif.)--Biography.
Classification: LCC CT1458.A56 A3 2018 (ebook) | LCC CT1458.A56 (print) | DDC
 306.874/3--dc23
LC record available at https://lccn.loc.gov/2017057379

First Edition

10 9 8 7 6 5 4 3 2 1

Dedication

To my mother,
Zora Marinovič Amochaev

Acknowledgments

This is a story based on memory about the Balkans, a land where even facts disagree. It reflects one version of a history of conflict, war, and exile.

As I write this, my adopted country struggles with issues of acceptance of immigrants and refugees, and conflicts between radically differing beliefs.

I am grateful to the people of the United States of America for accepting my family and giving me the opportunities to forge a life I cherish.

Table of Contents

SOCIALIST FEDERAL REPUBLIC
OF YUGOSLAVIA
AS OF 1 JANUARY 1991

CHAPTER ONE
Going home

"Of course I can find the home I was born in!" Mama exclaimed, in response to his question.

Climbing a hill that rose sharply from the Adriatic Sea, we three seekers wandered, lost, on rough roads past ancient stone houses in the nearly deserted village in Croatia.

One of the pilgrims, Zora, my seventy-year-old widowed mother, was in a town she had left as an infant. She was searching for the home she was born in, for the house in which she believed her uncle still lived. I walked with her, able to communicate with the people, for Mama had always insisted that her language was my birthright and would not be lost to me. My American husband Harold—the third pilgrim—spoke only English but was first to understand the challenges of our situation.

1

"Well, where is your house then, Zora?" he asked.

"It is near here; I am sure of that. I just need to look a little longer, Harold."

"Zora, we've walked up and down every road in this village . . ."

"I know," she interrupted, "but I can see it in my mind as clearly as if it were yesterday."

"Okay, Okay, I give up." Harold smiled and put his arm around her. "If you aren't tired, we can keep going."

Mama looked at my tall husband with a bemused expression. She always insisted her height was five feet and a half. That half was only half an inch, but Zora was anybody's equal. English was her third or fourth language, depending on how much of a language you needed to know to count it. She spoke it well, but with a Slavic accent.

He was blond, blue-eyed, six feet six inches tall without shoes. English was his first—and only— language. He didn't really know where in Germany his family had come from, or when. It had never seemed important.

Personally, I was afraid we were at an impasse. I knew that in Mama's mind, the house of her birth was a sacrosanct memory. I knew because it had been featured in so many of the stories she had told me of her life and her childhood. I felt that I could almost find that home myself.

But this was her search for her past, and nothing was jelling. I was staying out of this phase of the discussion. Harold knew how to avoid pushing the buttons that I always seemed to land on. Ours was a mother-daughter friction developed over the stresses of a lifetime, while theirs was a uniquely close relationship for a man and his mother-in-law.

This trip represented an important turning point in our lives. Zora had been struggling since the death of my father a few years earlier. Diminished and listless, her step had lost its bounce; her eyes their challenge. She rarely went out, and didn't want to venture far when she did.

Then, unexpectedly, she decided it was time to reconnect with her family home. "*Ti znaš, Tania*" she said to me, "*ne možemo više čekati.* You know, Tania, we can't wait forever for this war to end." That sentence of Zora's was a key milestone, and Harold and I quickly moved to support her desire.

Unfortunately, Zora's personal struggles had come neither at the beginning nor the end of the problems for her troubled Balkan homeland. At the time of our visit, in 1992, the Balkans were once again at war. It seemed this one would destroy the country of Yugoslavia for good.

A few months earlier Harold and I had been sitting in the kitchen where I had spent my childhood. Mama served her personal version of *doboš torta* — a dessert she had baked for Harold — while I translated a letter from my Aunt Slavića in Serbia. Mama's six sisters and their families were spread throughout Serbia and Croatia and she watched in horror, helpless, as their world crumbled around them. But Slavića closed her letter not with her loathing of the war, but with the joy of being close to her family and her many grandchildren. That, more than anything else, seemed to reach Zora.

Of course we did not want to head directly into the war zone, and would have to wait a few years before we felt it was safe to visit Mama's sisters deep in the current battlegrounds. But after significant consideration and discussion, we decided we could safely explore the northwestern tip of Croatia — Istria — a peninsula just across from Venice. It was a part of the country that had not seen any fighting. More importantly, it was also where Mama was born.

We would go see the house where her parents — my grandparents — had lived. We would try to find her uncle, and reconnect with a part of her family that she had left as an infant.

"Remember, Tania," Mama reminded me, of my own journey to the place we had lived when I was a baby. "How you found Campo, that awful refugee camp in Trieste, where we all lived? It was when you were in college and went back to Trieste. Now I can show you where my family lived when I was little."

I started thinking about the possibility of experiencing her country, her homeland, with Mama. I found myself wondering why we had never done it before. After all, I was already in my forties, and she was seventy. Now that we were going, I could hardly wait to see it through her eyes, and share her stories while in her home. I also hoped it would help pull her out of the deep sadness she had fallen into with the loss of my father.

A few weeks later Harold and I sat in the back of a taxi, with Zora and the driver in front. We were heading south from Trieste along the Adriatic Coast on the Istrian peninsula, perhaps the most beautiful part of Croatia. The small village of Medulin, our destination, was located near the city of Pula, at its southern tip. We were in a taxi for the hundred-kilometer trip because no rental car company was willing to let us cross the border from calm to chaos in their vehicle. Croatia had declared independence from what remained of Yugoslavia, the place once listed as the country of birth on my passport. The war of dissolution was ongoing.

Yugoslavia was a land that might well have been overlooked based only on size and population, but instead it ignited the spark that had led to World War I. It played a role in Germany's loss of World War II, and it was closing this same century at war with itself. The taxi driver quickly made the complexity of the situation we were heading into more personal.

He told us that he was himself a Serb who had fled the wars, one of many who had landed in Trieste. He and Mama spent the entire trip discussing the situation. Mama talked of her sisters in Serbia and Croatia, for both of them had families still in the midst of the fighting. I translated sparingly for Harold, afraid he might not be entirely confident of our decision to make this trip. The driver confirmed that our destination, in Istria, was remote from the embattled areas and was removed from the direct crisis. He, at least, was confident we would be safe in our search for Mama's roots. In that taxi, we didn't yet know that the challenges would lie in the search itself.

The taxi dropped us at the Hotel Brioni, in the city of Pula. Perched on the coastline, it was near the summer estate of Marshal Josip Broz Tito, the leader of Yugoslavia until his death in 1980. In its glory the

Brioni had reigned proudly, but now, rundown and nearly empty, it was a far cry from the Old-World grace of the Savoia Palace in Trieste, where we had started the journey. Nothing here had been maintained in a long time; perhaps not since the communists took over Yugoslavia after World War II, and certainly not since the present conflicts had started in the late 1980s. Things looked grim as we then headed out to rent a local car. No tourists were interested in taking a trip into this unsettled situation. No crowds would stand between us and our idea of finding Zora's house.

The town of Medulin was just a few miles from Pula. We at first encountered scenes that had certainly not existed at Zora's birth. What had once been a charming beach was now littered with Communist-style dilapidated buildings, hotels that looked like high-rise slums. The people milling around clearly weren't on holiday. We learned later that many Croatian refugees from the conflict had been given shelter at this waterside resort area, and that it had become an informal refugee camp.

We continued along the waterfront road, then turned inland, toward the old town.

Zora had come to life as we traveled south from Trieste. When we approached the center of Medulin, she told me which way to turn, when to keep going. She had suddenly been transformed back into the strong woman I used to know — energized and confident.

The town, in contrast, was quiet and nearly empty. It was seemingly untouched by the uncontrolled development and crowding near the water. Continuing upward along the hill, we parked the car near the top and started exploring, relying on Zora to lead us to her home.

The houses around us were built of local stone; vines grew on old wooden arbors and gates. The roads were no longer all dirt, as they had been when Mama was young, but they were run-down, crumbling along the edges, merging with weeds and rocks. A cemetery surrounded the small church at the top of the hill. Mama's parents grew up thinking they would be buried there, as would their children. But it didn't happen that way.

Zora led us up and down several roads, sometimes pausing with a distant look in her eyes to touch a wall or stare at a door. She had left there as an infant and was searching for the house she was born in, one in which she believed her uncle still lived.

She kept looking. Many houses matched the image in her mind, but she was searching for *her* home.

Had she assumed that she would breathe the air as she approached her mother's house, and, like a baby calmed only by her mother's milk — unique, unlike any other mother's milk — she would recognize it?

But she didn't.

Harold started feeling uncomfortable. We were, after all, in a war-torn country, one that didn't seem warm and friendly to him. It felt strangely abandoned, almost derelict. He was the first to acknowledge the challenges of our situation and question Zora directly.

"Weren't you just a baby when you left this area?" he asked as it became clear we were not going to find the house.

"I was, Harold. We escaped after the First World War, when Mussolini took over. But I went back with my mother, just after the Second World War, in the late 1940s."

"How long did you spend here on that visit?"

"Oh, I only had a few days off from my work. It was short."

"Zora, even that was almost fifty years ago."

I could feel her mind sifting through a lifetime of events.

Everything had changed.

Nothing had changed.

Here she was, back where it all started: a widow with her own daughter and son-in-law, visiting a country that was again at war. Her country— splintering back to the divisions that last existed at the time of her birth.

"I remember it was a short walk," she said. "Straight up the hill from the center of town. The church was at the top of the road, the sea at the bottom. We just have to find the right road."

The problem, I finally understood, was that this description of the small road with the church at the top and the sea below fit almost every road of this town on its small hill.

"Do you have their address?" Harold asked. "Did you correspond?"

"Correspond?" she said, looking at me.

Harold rephrased his question. "Did you write each other?"

He had to do that more and more with Zora. Even though she understood English quite well, some expressions escaped her. And her comprehension had recently started slipping.

"Oh, you know, I don't write letters. And my family is worse." Zora turned to me, and switched languages, as she often did. "*Kaži mu*, tell him, that there were no addresses. It was a small town. You just used people's names."

"So you know their name?" Harold asked.

"Of course I know their name! It's my uncle's family we're talking about." She slapped him gently, and she laughed. "Could you forget your uncle's name?"

"Sometimes I wonder," he said, a bit obscurely. I could tell he was starting to question what Zora really did remember. "I guess I'm just nervous wandering around a foreign country, near a war zone, not speaking the language."

"But this isn't a foreign country, Harold. This is my country."

That simple statement said so much. I wondered then what Mama was really looking for in coming here right now. My father's death had hit her extremely hard, and she hadn't been able to recover back at home. Here she seemed renewed. Was she reexamining her life in America? Did this explain her re-energized demeanor?

She was in a place she had left as an infant and visited only once again in her youth, but for Mama this clearly didn't feel foreign. They all spoke her language; their dialect was one that lived deep in her memory. The waters of the Adriatic sparkled around us, the harbor below was still full of fishing boats, and the coffee came black and thick in small ceramic cups.

But no matter how familiar it all seemed to her, we were hopelessly lost. No matter what she was seeking, we weren't finding it.

"Let's drive down to where the shops are, at the bottom of the hill, where we came in," I finally said, frustrated. "There was a café there, and some men were sitting outside."

We drove to the center of town. It was nearly deserted, with only a few people near the shops. A young woman stood outside the door of the café and pushed her baby carriage back and forth. An older woman emerged with a cake box and they walked away together. Suddenly I saw the post office.

"They probably have a phone book in there, and we can try searching in it," I suggested.

The post office was open, but, like everything else, seemed almost abandoned. Finally a young woman appeared at the counter.

"Can I help you?" she asked in Serbo-Croatian. Zora had spoken it with me all my life, insisting that her language was my birthright. She said we spoke *po našemu*. It meant in our way. In our language.

"We're looking for my mother's uncle, who lives here," I replied, *po našemu*. "Do you have a phone book?"

"Certainly." She understood me without a problem. "It's a bit old. We haven't had a new one since the war started. Has he lived here long?"

"Over eighty years," replied Zora, laughing. "Bogdan wouldn't move from here if you put a gun to his head." It wasn't perhaps the best figure of speech, given how her own father had left, but it got the point across.

There was no Bogdan Rojnič listed for Medulin. We also found no listing for Matte, Bogdan's son.

"I am sure we got letters from them," said Zora. "But that was before we left Yugoslavia."

"Ah . . . Did you live here, as well?" the young woman asked.

"Oh, I was born right here, in Medulin. My father was Martin Marinovič; my mother was Katarina Rojnič before she married. Bogdan was her brother. Their families lived here for centuries. But I left when I was very young," Mama continued, turning back to us. "I can't imagine what happened to Bogdan."

"Do you have a mailman who might know the local families?" I asked. "Maybe someone older?"

"There is an older mailman, but he has gone for lunch. He will be back around three."

"Thank you," I said, relieved at this new possibility. "We'll come back."

We walked over to the café, got some coffee and some *torte*. The local cakes were very familiar to all of us, as Mama had baked them all my life. As we sat down the young woman suddenly came out from the post office, looked around, and then approached the outside table where we were sitting.

"*Izvinite, molim vas*. I'm so sorry," she said, flustered. "I just remembered. He won't be back this afternoon. He finished his rounds early and has gone fishing for the weekend. You can talk to him next week."

Her words were devastating. Next week we would be on a ferry to Venice. It looked like our chance of finding what we came for — Mama's family home and her relatives — was evaporating.

It had seemed so achievable, this plan to stop in a town just across the water from Venice and find Mama's home. Now we just sat and stared at each other.

"Tell us what you remember," Harold finally said to Zora. He wanted to learn as much as possible about this quiet spot where her story began, and about those who stayed when her family was forced to leave. Maybe it would lead us somewhere.

I looked at Mama, trying to imagine her thoughts, barely knowing my own.

"*Ne razumem ništa.* I don't understand anything. In my mind it was all so clear," Zora finally said. "When I was a girl, my mother talked about Istria all the time. About how hard it was for her to have to leave. About their life here."

"A lot like you talked about my childhood with me when I was younger, right, Mama?"

"That's right, Tania."

"It's the reason I can remember life in Trieste, from when I was a baby. You talked about it so often," I said, referring to my own young childhood. Because of my Mama's stories, I knew what it was like to have vivid memories of a time when I was very young.

"Yes, that's right, Tania. And of course you found Campo when you went back. I was sure I would find my Mama's home, too." She and I talked, *po našemu*, in our language, while I translated for Harold. It was a familiar mode; we could have been back in Zora's kitchen in San Francisco.

"I remember being in her kitchen so clearly," Zora continued. "She would cook dinner, I did my schoolwork and helped my sisters with theirs."

"Mama talked about the time when I was born," Zora was in full storytelling mode. "About living across the street from Roža and Bogdan. About your grandfather, *Deda Marinovič,* fishing. About purple grapes and ripe figs. She was convinced that the days were clearer, that nature was celebrating the end of war. That life was getting better. But it wasn't to be, you know." Zora's voice drifted off as she visualized a past she only knew through her mother's voice. She could hear it as if Katarina was with us in that moment, in Medulin, talking to her. *Po našemu.*

For Katarina had always told stories to her daughters when they were young, painting a picture of life right there, in Istria. Zora heard about a woman in love with her husband, her children, and with her beautiful homeland. But there was always a hidden tension to the stories, for Zora knew how they ended, and that nothing was as simple as Katarina's telling made it sound. For Zora, her mother's stories — with Venetian ships, wars, an ogre called Mussolini, and threats of exile — were riveting, and she never grew tired of listening, especially her favorite story: the one about her. The one about the baby that couldn't wait.

"Our lives changed when you were born," Katarina would tell little Zora. These stories often started with the words: "*Sve se opet promjenilo.* Nothing was ever the same again."

PART I

Katarina

CHAPTER TWO

The baby who wouldn't wait

"Ova ne čeka. This one won't wait," were the words that always got Zora listening, because that story was about her.

It was the summer of 1922, the grapes were still green, the figs just ripening, and the fish were hiding farther out at sea than usual as Katarina struggled with the approaching birth of her seventh child. The First World War was over, and new babies had already come tumbling into their world. Four girls filled the house with noise; the two lost boys were still missed.

In their small town of Medulin they perched on a hill overlooking the Adriatic, a sea she would never tire of watching, even when the Bura winds howled over it toward Italy. Katerina knew the massive stones used to build their houses would keep them warm and safe from the fiercest storms.

Prokleti Italiani, she thought. It was the damned Italians, not the winds, threatening them now. Just a few years ago it had been the Hungarians, and before that the Austrians. It was always someone. Endless wars. Perhaps the beauty of their homeland was so irresistible the fighting over its control would never end.

This baby, the seventh she would bear, wasn't due until August, but Katarina had known she wouldn't wait. She always knew when they would be girls, and it was no different with this one.

"*Ova neče dugo čekati,* Martin," she had said to her husband as he was getting ready to go out to sea a few days earlier. "This one won't wait much longer."

"Luckily Roža can help when you need it," he replied. They were at home, across the road from Katarina's childhood house, where her brother Bogdan lived with his wife Roža and their young son. Martin was happy that Roža was a good midwife. She had taken care of Katarina through Slavića's traumatic birth after the war's end. He knew she would take care of Katarina now, while he was gone. "I really have to go out for a few days on this ship, you know."

"Yes, I know, but I still worry about you going out, Martin." Every time he left she felt uneasy. "It's not over yet, is it?"

"Not really. And no ships will protect us . . ." Martin caught himself. He didn't need to talk about it just now. "I'll be back soon, *duša*, my soul. Everything will be all right."

Martin knew it wasn't looking good. World War I was long over, yet the spoils were still being fought over, and their home was in the middle of it all. But he didn't want to worry Katarina just now. She had been slowly getting over her personal tragedies from that last war, going forward day by day, remembering anew how wonderful their life here had always been. He couldn't bear to have her frightened again. There would be time to talk about it when he returned. He had some plans to work out in the meantime.

Katarina was right. The baby really couldn't wait to get out. A few days after Martin left she sat in Roža's kitchen, looking out the window at her own home. Martin was still out to sea; Bogdan was at work. Babies and children ran around outside in the open courtyard, near the vegetable garden. She could hear the pig grunting and the chickens pecking in their enclosure. The *jezva*, the old copper Turkish coffee pot, was on the wood stove, still hot from the midday meal. Aromas of strong coffee mingled with ripe fruit smells. A bee buzzed in through the open door, mistaking the flowers in the old clay jug for the ones growing outside.

Katarina had grown up in this kitchen; she still knew it better than Roža did. How many generations of women had cooked Turkish coffee the same way on that same stove? How many had waited here for their babies, imagining the lives to come? She was just slipping into a gentle reverie as Roža bustled back in from picking tomatoes.

That was when she felt the first pains. She gripped the table before her, its wood polished by her own mother's hands, its edges rounded from years of use. The olive tree out in back, the one that had replaced the one this table was crafted from, was already ancient in its own right. It felt good to hold on to something she had known since childhood, to ground herself as this new baby pushed her way into the world.

July 21 it was, the heart of that warm summer of 1922. Roža got her across the road to her own bed, the one she shared with her beloved Martin. The place where she had given birth so many times already, and where he himself had been born.

The new one was born a few hours later, before her father came back from his voyage. Of course it was a girl, and she literally burst into the world, as if she knew her parents were counting on her to bring in a new dawn.

"*Pa koliko je ljepa.* My, she's so beautiful," breathed Martin a few days later, when he saw her.

"You think they are all beautiful," Katarina said, happy he was home. Back with her. Safe.

"That's because they are all beautiful."

My beautiful wife and my beautiful babies, he thought. *I should feel like the luckiest man in the whole universe!*

If only it was that simple.

CHAPTER THREE

Surviving the First War

Martin often looked back on his life and remembered what came before the birth of his seventh child. His mind coursed back over the years, and all the challenges they had lived through. But there was one story he never shared. It was the story of a time just after the First World War, when there had been only four children, and of Katarina coming back from her forced exile during that war.

Thirty-five at the war's onset in 1914, Martin was too old to fight, and in any case, his maritime building expertise was vital to the war effort. He was conscripted to work at the military shipyard in the nearby city of Pula, where the Austro-Hungarian Empire had its naval shipyards. The very existence of that naval center made it dangerous for families to stay in the area, especially after Italy joined the war on the side of the British. The enemy was suddenly next door.

Their Austrian rulers were now surrounded by enemies, and worried about potential traitors within. They decided to deport wives and families. But they needed the shipyard workers to stay loyal, so they told Martin and his colleagues that their families were being evacuated for their own safety rather than as security against their potential treason. No one was given a choice; they were simply told to bring one suitcase each and be at the train station in the morning.

So the women and children had been sent *negde daleko* – somewhere far away – supposedly somewhere safe. The men knew their families had been moved east, into what was then Hungary, but there had been virtually no contact since their evacuation in 1915. Martin grew ever more desperate as time passed without word from Katarina, but there was nothing he could do but wait.

When the war finally ended three years later Martin and his colleagues returned to their empty homes and started rebuilding their lives, waiting for their families to return. A single letter reached Martin's brother-in-law, Bogdan, telling him that the women were on their way. At last.

But the Katarina who had left—a strong, vibrant woman with two sons and two daughters—was not the same woman who returned. A radically altered Katarina—a woman with only two children, their daughters Mara and Rožića—got off the train.

Martin couldn't sort through his emotions: relief at his wife's arrival, shock at everything else. Katarina had changed frighteningly while in exile. Her hair was still nearly black, but her eyes didn't have the sparkle Martin had fallen in love with as a young man. Her face was lined, and she walked like some of the soldiers he had seen upon their return from battle—bent over, huddled into herself, looking around furtively. Even the girls—who had still been babies on their departure—re-entered his life as quiet, oddly adult-like children trailing behind their mother.

Martin reached out his powerful arms and held Katarina gently. He knelt to encircle the girls. Tears poured down Katarina's face as she told him that the two boys got sick and were taken away. She was told they had caught the flu.

"*Nisu se vratili, duše. Nema ih.* They didn't return, dear. They are gone."

Their sons had been taken away to a quarantine center with hundreds of others and had not come home. Katarina never saw her boys again. The authorities didn't even pretend to understand her language. She was simply told that they had died and were buried. She and the girls were not allowed anywhere near the quarantine areas for fear of the infection spreading. At that time, Katarina didn't know that the flu epidemic raged across the continent in 1918 and killed nearly fifty million people—more than even the war. She only knew her sons were gone, and that many women lost children. It was almost always, it seemed to her, the boys.

And then the Hungarian military was routed, evacuating and abandoning territory, left with but a small fraction of their earlier lands. It was a chaotic time. The soldiers rampaged and destroyed randomly, rather than leave anything for the enemy, and the women and children always felt afraid and helpless. The conditions were worse than even during the war, but Katarina didn't want to leave, convinced her boys were still there, somewhere. She never believed they had died. In the end, though, attacked by the fleeing troops, fearing for her very life, she had no choice but to run.

Katarina was afraid the nightmares would never end, but then she found just enough strength to gather her girls and forget everything else. She locked it all deep in a person who no longer existed, focused on making it home and nothing more.

Martin could barely take it all in. He had lost his sons, and now he felt there was a risk of losing his wife as well. She seemed on the verge of losing her mind. He had to be strong for all of them so they could rebuild their lives in this beautiful spot that he knew so well.

Katarina and Martin's families had lived in Medulin, just across the Adriatic Sea from Venice, for centuries. Originally their *pradjedi*, their ancestors, had come from the coast of Montenegro, in the southern Balkans, near Albania and Serbia.

"The Marinovič clan were always shipbuilders," Martin would say when it was his turn to tell the children stories. He talked of the Venetians sending big ships south, after their population was wiped out by the plagues of the Middle Ages. He himself had grown up on stories about those ships, of how they were seaworthy, large and beautiful. The people were told of a fertile land that would be welcoming. Venice promised jobs rebuilding the shipyard in Pula, and guaranteed that they could speak their own language.

In Montenegro, meanwhile, the Ottoman Empire fought constantly to subjugate the population. Wars

continued around them for centuries with little res-
pite. The Montenegrins were fierce fighters who used
their harsh landscape to confound the conquest. But it
was always a brutal existence. Finally their ancestors
couldn't resist the opportunity; they boarded those
big ships and left their land behind.

It was a good life they had found here. A life very
different, and in so many ways easier than the ones
their ancestors had endured on the hard rocky coast
of Montenegro. On this sheltered peninsula, with the
fish and the warm climate, they were never hungry,
never too cold. Summer brought figs and grapes,
winter the root vegetables. The cellars under the
houses kept the potatoes fresh and the wine cold.
And in the late autumn they could go into the hills
and pick mushrooms, or even better, the wonderful
dark brown globules of truffle.

Venetian rule lasted a few hundred years, then
Napoleon defeated them and briefly took over. But
he traded the area to Austria in exchange for the
Netherlands, and by the 1800s it was the Austro-
Hungarian Empire that controlled the land, incorpo-
rating it into Croatia. It was the only government
young Katarina and Martin knew, and they really
didn't have much to do with any government. Their
town was too small for anyone to bother them. And
through all these changes, for hundreds of years,

their Slavic language was protected. Everyone around them spoke *po našemu*, in their way, a dialect evolving from Serbian and Croatian.

Katarina and Martin grew up across the road from each other, in old stone houses deeply embedded in that land. They knew each other all their lives, but they were the first to tie the two families in marriage.

During the early years of the century, Martin, like his ancestors, worked as a shipbuilder in Pula, by then the primary port of the Austro-Hungarian navy. A five-mile walk from his home, it held much of Austria's fleet, a fact that gained enormous significance with one fateful event.

On June 28, 1914, Gavrilo Princip, the nineteen-year-old son of a Bosnian Serb postman, walked out of a sandwich shop in Sarajevo, deep in the Balkans, onto the street where a car carrying Archduke Franz Ferdinand, heir to the Austrian throne, was backing up, having made a wrong turn. The world was never the same again. The assassination of the Archduke by Gavrilo Princip launched World War I.

The Balkans ignited the fighting, but this was a battle for the domination of Europe by Germany and Austria against Britain, France and Russia.

Istria itself was no more than a dot on the map of that conflagration. But the results of the war had an outsized effect on the Slavs who lived on this small peninsula, and life would change irrevocably for Martin and Katarina.

Italy had been expected to enter World War I on the side of Austria and Germany. Instead, in 1915, the country signed a secret treaty with Britain which promised that portions of the Dalmatian Coast, and, most important to Katarina and her family, the entire peninsula of Istria, would go to Italy if the Allies prevailed. In addition to providing deep-water ports, the Dalmatian coast — with Istria at its northern edge and Dubrovnik to the south — is blessed with clear water, jagged cliffs, picturesque islands, and beautiful small seaports. It could also open the door to eastern trade routes. Italy desperately wanted this land.

Martin didn't want to remember those hard years of war, of building and repairing ships for armies he wished would all sink to the bottom of the sea. Whether the winners were the Italians or the British or the Austrians or the Germans, he wanted nothing to do with any of them. And mostly, he just wanted his family back.

Eventually it became clear Germany would lose the war. Then the Austro-Hungarian Empire dissolved. The women would soon be home. But Martin didn't know what country they would return to.

CHAPTER FOUR
Balkanization

A brief look at history could help clarify why this question lay so heavy on Martin's mind.

For most of the world a simple geographic descriptor—the Balkans—paints a picture of impenetrable chaos. This was the part of the world that included the Marinovič heritage—both Medulin and Montenegro. That very word, Balkanization, describes things crumbling, disintegrating, dissolving—again and again and again. The word first appeared in the early 1800s, but took firm hold after World War I, as Martin and Katarina were trying to find their way forward. Unknown to them, it would apply for over a century, growing more toxic over time.

The land known as the Balkans—an area the size of France, and including Croatia, Serbia, Montenegro and Slovenia as well as parts of Greece, Bulgaria and Hungary — was the location of Europe's first advanced civilizations, beginning with the Bronze Age around 3200 BC. It was where the Greek and Roman Empires met — with the Roman, or Latin, influence coming from the north and west, the Greek, later Byzantine, influence coming from the east and south. Even today, Serbian and Croatian, virtually a single language, use two different alphabets — Serbian the Byzantine-influenced Cyrillic and Croatian the Roman-sourced Latin.

Bronze Age tools are found regularly in hill towns of the area and Pula boasts an almost intact enormous Roman gladiatorial arena. But like a high school prom queen who bloomed too soon, that was the end of the golden era.

By the Middle Ages, the wars between the Byzantine and Roman empires had already launched hundreds of years of nearly unremitting conflict. When those two empires finally dissolved, the Ottoman Turks created a new cataclysm for the region, one that started in the thirteenth century and ended only with the First World War. During that period, with the development of modern Europe focused primarily toward the west, the Balkans suffered hundreds of years of conquest, depopulation and cultural stagnation. Whenever the Turks were defeated in one area, it seemed, there was another conqueror ready to step in: the Venetian Empire; Napoleon and the French; the Austro-Hungarian Empire. All these conquests brought political dominance, but also a different religion, a different language—with its concomitant alphabets—and a different culture. There was no end of outside powers—just as there was no end to a desire by the dominated peoples for self-rule.

And finally, as the First World War was ending, they had their chance. Southern Slavic nationalists called for independence and unification. The people of these countries didn't always like each other, but they hated a common enemy more: any outside power that tried to defeat and control them. It was a Serb whose action started the war that had now freed the Croats and Slovenes of their Austro-Hungarian overlords. But Serbia had paid a high price: they had the highest casualties per capita in the war. It was enough. They overlooked their differences and bonded together, in desperation and fear of what might be done to them if they didn't. For it was again the outside powers—the Americans, the English and the French—who were deciding postwar boundaries.

In December of 1918, before the Treaty of Versailles was finalized, an improbable but almost inevitable union of countries with embattled histories was proclaimed in Belgrade as the Kingdom of Serbs, Croats and Slovenes. It was an incredible, independent act of self-determination that occurred in spite of all the outside powers. The United States quickly recognized the Kingdom. And the Austrians, in their retreat, granted their naval headquarters to this new Kingdom rather than hand it over to the enemy, Italy.

Martin and his co-workers celebrated when the shipyard in Pula was ceded along with the entire Austrian fleet to this newly formed union, this Kingdom of Serbs, Croats, and Slovenes. Their kingdom. Its awkward name would soon evolve to Yugoslavia—from the words *yugo*, or southern, and *Slav*.

They continued repairing war-damaged ships and there was talk of building new ones, but this time for their own people. However, conflicting news reports swirled around them endlessly, with talk of treaties, discussions in Versailles, debates over country boundaries, the creation of a League of Nations—uncertainty about the future. How long would this good news last?

Martin couldn't understand why it was so hard to figure it all out. They were all Slavs here, certainly it made sense they should be part of the new Kingdom. But now that the fighting had ended, happy as he was that they had gained ownership of their country, he just wanted to be back with his wife, his Katarina.

She wouldn't talk about what happened to her there, *negde daleko*, somewhere far away, while she and her children were in exile. She never did.

And then, suddenly, there was to be another child. Too soon. Martin feared for Katarina, for how recent her losses were. He trembled at the thought of the tragedy that had taken place, the violation she had endured while she was away from his protection. Ultimately, though, he saw that only love — for the new child and for each other — would help them move forward. No one would ever replace the boys, but they could start rebuilding the family.

Just before her labors started, Katarina grabbed Martin's hand in a grip so tight that a big red spot formed over his middle knuckle. "Promise me, Martin," she whispered, looking deeply into his eyes, terrified of what she might see there, "that you will love this one as much as you love the rest."

Her dark eyes looked through Martin as she spoke, and he knew she was seeing far beyond him. He could hardly breathe for the pain that shot through him, but spoke calmly, knowing that only the reassurance of his deep love could bring her back to him.

"Oh, Kata, Kata, *ljubov moja*, my love," One tear—the only one she was ever to see on that wind-hardened face—ran down his cheek. "I will love her as much as I love you, *draga, draga moja*." And he knew, right then, that it was true. That he would look at this child and always feel the gratitude of finding his family again.

Martin wasn't far away, on that first day of 1919, when the new baby came squalling into the world. He could hardly bear to leave the room, terrified that something would go wrong, that he might lose his precious Katarina.

Slava, they called that child—Glory—Slavića in the diminutive, and she was indeed a glorious baby who brought joy to their lives. She patched them back together, this little human weighing barely over seven pounds, and they started moving forward, trying to put those awful years out of their memories.

CHAPTER FIVE

Post war crises

Like Katarina, many of the women and children in the small town of Medulin had been deported to Hungary for the duration of the war. They were all trying to return to a normal life. While the memory of her two young sons would torture Katarina for the rest of her life, she did finally move on, with the support of her Martin—her sweet Martin, whose warm body wrapped itself around hers, whose embraces, as they moved from gentle to passionate, gave her such deep comfort, even when the newest baby was still young. She knew what it would lead to. But she loved those new soft warm bodies next to hers as much as she loved his hard one.

Little Jana followed Slavića's birth by just over a year. And then in the summer of 1922, the birth of another child, Katarina's seventh, approached. It was the baby that wouldn't wait.

Katarina was developing a renewed love for her home — for the sea breezes that blew up the hill and swirled around the top before moving on toward Italy, cooling off the mainland. For her brother Bogdan and his wife Roža, just across the road. It was a good life they thought they were rebuilding on that sheltered coast.

But while the war was over, the battle for peace continued unabated in the Marinovic family's part of the world. It would be a long time before borders were finalized and the implications fully understood. If life were fair, Medulin and the Marinovič family, also Southern Slavs, would stay part of that new federation, moving into a new future. But the secret treaty signed between Italy and Great Britain, the one that had brought the Italians in on the right side of the war, had promised the Dalmatian coast to Italy. And Istria was to prove pivotal to that commitment.

Italy would not get its promised Dalmatia. Croatia would stay in the Kingdom, now called Yugoslavia. But by early 1920 a new treaty gave Italy control of one small but key part of that land: the Istrian peninsula. Suddenly the future was not so clear. They were to be ruled by the Italians. How could it be that one more time they were under a foreign power? What would happen to them now?

At first not much changed. The shipyard continued briefly under Yugoslavia, as the entire Austro-Hungarian naval and merchant fleet had been ceded to them. The flag on the post office was replaced by the Italian one, and government offices in Pula were swiftly changed out. Life in the countryside was hardly affected until a new name started appearing in the news.

Mussolini, a man whose significance was not yet understood by the outside world, was gaining power and consolidating his position in Italy. He started acting quickly and quietly to assert Italian dominance over this new area and its populace. Mussolini's influence would eventually touch everyone in Istria deeply, for he publicly spoke of his hatred of Slavs.

As the implications of those events became more apparent, with Slavic schools closing and Italian families moving in, Martin grew frightened, concerned that they were being pushed out of their home. And where could they go? That *prokleti rat,* damned war. That *prokleti* Mussolini. For the rest of Europe, for America, it was over. But not for them. Here, it seemed it might never end. If, or more probably when, Mussolini consolidated his growing power in Italy, he would act decisively to rid himself of the Slavs, whom he viewed as interlopers on *his* land.

"We need to talk, *draga*." Martin said one evening in that summer of 1922, when the baby was getting close. He was clearly under stress, and knew it was only a matter of time before he had no work, as the shipyard was in the process of being transferred to the Italians.

"We can't stay here worrying about our lives. I've been thinking about moving, even if only for a time, to where we can feel safe, where I can find work, where we can speak our language."

Martin hadn't told Katarina that when Bogdan went down to enter his son's name in the birth records at the church, Father Carlo suggested they write the Italian name Milan, as well as the name they had chosen, Matte. Bogdan didn't want trouble and followed the advice. But their son would be Matte at home, where it mattered, and Bogdan didn't want to worry Roža about it. Besides, there were bigger issues to deal with. Their very way of life was at stake.

"What are you saying?" Katarina asked.

"Mussolini hates all Slavs, and it looks like he will soon be in charge," Martin said. "Bogdan has heard he wants us out of here. He's moving in Italian families, taking over whole villages. Bogdan thinks they're going to try to ban our language."

"Our language? How can they do that?"

"They can, believe me, they can," said Martin. "Bogdan thinks we should just live quietly, without complaint. He doesn't believe it will actually come to this. After all, our people have lived here in peace for hundreds of years."

"And you, Martin?"

"I'll be damned if some Italian puppetmaster is going to force me to give up my soul," cursed Martin. "This house was built by the ancestors of my ancestors. It was here before Mussolini was born, and it will be here long after he dies. Did we fight a war just to have it taken from under us by this false peace?"

"Please be careful what you say, Martin. Bogdan might have the right idea; just let them think you are going along with them."

"I'll be careful, Katarina," he said. "But it might not stop with the language. Mussolini might take our homes, our jobs, everything. That's why I think it is time to consider where we might escape to, *mila moja*, my dear one. Thank goodness the Yugoslavian union was created just in time. I think we can be safe there."

"You're frightening me, Martin. I can't bear to think about leaving here ever again. Once was enough. I want us to stay. Things have been getting better here since the war ended. Besides, this baby is all I can worry about right now. It should be a joyous time for us, Martin. The beginning of a new life. Please," Katarina continued, "let's talk about her name."

"I know the name!" Martin exclaimed. His face lit up, and he seemed to put his worries behind him for at least a moment. Maybe Katarina was right, and they could stay. But either way, he was ready to move forward with their lives. "If it's a girl she will be *Zora*, the dawn, and if it's a boy, Zoran. In spite of how things look, maybe it can be a new dawn, a new day, even for us. I know we can make a new future for our family."

Zora, thought Katarina. This was the perfect name for the child who could help them usher in a new life. Zora would be the first in their family to have a name picked for her by her father. She would mostly be called Zorića, since everyone always used diminutive names in the family, and it was an adorable nickname.

Martin left soon after this conversation, thinking he would be back before the baby was born. He had one last trip to take as the commercial ships were leaving,

44

and he had to solidify his prospects so he could talk to Katarina about the future with confidence.

P.N.F. - Comando Squadristi - Dignano

Attenzione!

Si proibisce nel modo più assoluto che nei ritrovi pubblici e per le strade di Dignano si canti o si parli in lingua slava.

Anche nei negozi di qualsiasi genere deve essere una buona volta adoperata

SOLO LA LINGUA ITALIANA

Noi Squadristi, con metodi persuasivi, faremo rispettare il presente ordine.

GLI SQUADRISTI

A leaflet from the period of Fascist Italianization prohibiting singing or speaking in the "Slavic language" in the streets and public places of Dignano (now Vodnjan, Croatia, near Pula in Istria). Signed by the Squadristi (blackshirts), and threatening the use of "persuasive methods" in enforcement.

CHAPTER SIX

Finding another way

Martin went out the door, waved to Bogdan, and walked down the hill. Perhaps it was the sorrow of losing it, but the village seemed more beautiful than ever. The stone houses were strong; there was lots of room for growing families, and plenty of space for the children to play. In the evenings they could sit in the courtyards and have a *rakija,* a homemade fruit brandy, or a sweet wine made from their own grapes.

He passed the parcels of land that had been in his family for centuries, as well as the new ones he had been acquiring, the land that was supposed to give his daughters an edge when they were searching for husbands. He didn't mind if the next baby was also a girl. Martin still ached at the loss of his boys, but there was no replacing them. At least girls wouldn't go fight, if it ever came to that again.

At the bottom of the hill lay the small harbor where the fishing fleet was based. Martin had helped build a number of those boats. He knew the ones that his father had built before him were also still seaworthy. Shipbuilding was in their blood. It had been that way for generations, for the name had come with them from their old homeland of Montenegro. Marinovič, it meant "of the sea." For all that time, since they left with the Venetian fleet, the Marinovič and Rojnič families had lived peacefully in Istria.

And now, after all these generations, we are being forced to flee again, Martin thought as he approached the commercial shipyard. The fact that the Turks had finally been defeated in the war only added to the tragic irony of the situation. Martin knew deep inside that he had to find an acceptable alternative, and he hoped he could confirm one on this trip.

He had considered Croatia, and even Montenegro. But there was nothing there for him. Croatia was uncomfortably close to Mussolini. Montenegro was not only politically unstable, it was very poor. Then he learned that the new commercial shipyards in Novi Sad and Petrovaradin, in Serbia, not too far from Belgrade, were hiring. This was mixed news, but held at least an opportunity for employment and for their future.

Serbia seemed to be a safe haven of this union, although no one could guarantee how things would evolve. Unfortunately, Novi Sad was actually in a part of eastern Serbia called Vojvodina, a so-called Autonomous Region still disputed between Yugoslavia and Hungary. But Martin was running out of options. He debated the alternatives but kept returning to this one and now traveled there to check it out.

Novi Sad, he found, was an attractive city on a wide sweep of the Danube river, not far from Belgrade. Better yet, Petrovaradin, across the river, was a village on the water, overlooked by an ancient Roman fortress, known as the Gibraltar of the Danube. Much like Medulin, it was on a hill rising above the water. Martin found a place where they could live. It was a small house on a dirt lane in Petrovaradin close to the Danube, with a vegetable garden and enough land for some pigs and goats. It was small and quiet, and he thought Katarina might eventually find peace there.

The only negative aspect was its proximity to Hungary — who of course wanted it back — but he felt it would stay secure in Yugoslavia, as the headquarters of the Yugoslavian Royal Air Force had just been moved there. Since the area was intersected by three great navigable rivers — the Danube, Sava and

Tisa—it was the home of several major shipyards, and there were many opportunities for his craft.

Martin knew Katarina still held out a hope for staying in Medulin, but he now had an alternative if that became impossible.

He reached Medulin to joyous news. The baby hadn't waited long enough for her father to get home. Zora had literally burst into the world, as if she could help her parents bring in a new dawn.

Katarina wished that a new future might be possible in their own home. Her Rojnič identity belonged with their brother Slavs. But it was not to be. There was no going back. Croatia was definitively split between Italy and Yugoslavia. It was with despair that she accepted that their part of Istria was going to Italy while the rest of the Dalmatian Coast to the south and east went to Yugoslavia.

They were now being persecuted in their own homes. Italy's anger over not receiving the entire Dalmatian Coast that it had been promised fueled the growth of Mussolini's National Fascist Party. The man was Prime Minister in all but official title, winning because he was a rabid nationalist. The consequences were awful. Martin and Katarina's language was soon officially banned. The commercial shipyards were closing; the naval one went to the Italians. There was no more work here for Martin. The trip he had just undertaken was to be the last from his home port. The boat he had sailed on never came back.

Martin couldn't help but feel a near despair at thinking about wrenching his family away from all this: their home, the warm waters, his fish, their families' lives for the past four hundred years. If there were any other way, he would have found it. But this was the end.

When he had gone to get the paperwork to register Zora's birth he learned of the new law: Slavic names of any kind could no longer be registered.

He quietly filled out the form. Father Carlo had suggested the Italian word for Dawn. And so, the birth of this new baby; her father Martin Marinovič, shipbuilder; her mother Katarina Marinovič, ex-Rojnič; was duly recorded. Martin didn't want to think what country would claim his daughter. He wished Istria could be its own country. Then she could be Zora Marinovič, citizen of Istria. But there was no such place.

"It's still a beautiful name, Martin." Father Carlo had tried to reassure him.

"Zora is the only name she will hear from me." Martin put down the pen and stared at the hand that had signed the document, as if it belonged to someone else. "Please don't tell anyone. I don't want Katarina worrying about this new development."

It was with a heavy heart that Martin returned to his family and his new daughter. For them, her name would be Zora, or Dawn, but only God could imagine what life was dawning for them.

That night, when the children had gone to sleep, Martin and Katarina — still tired from Zora's birth — sat by the stove in the kitchen, grateful for some moments of silence.

"*Ne možemo ostati, duša.* We can't stay here anymore." Martin said, quietly reaching across the table for her hand. "The boat works are closed."

"What? *Oj, joj, joj!*"

"Yes, the *vlasti*," he said, using the all-encompassing word for the powers-that-be, "in Belgrade have quietly moved almost all the boats out. It's definite; the Italians are in charge here, and they have commercial shipbuilding facilities along their own coast. I don't have any work."

And on October 31, 1922, Mussolini, the *de facto* leader for some time, was officially elected Prime Minister of Italy.

Mussolini quickly forced out as many of the Slavs as he could and settled Italians in their place. He fired all those who had worked for the government. The Slavic languages — both Slovenian and Croatian — were formally outlawed, the schools closed. The churches were already Catholic and the Masses said in Latin. Luckily, most of the prelates had been sent from the Vatican, and he quickly dispatched any who were Slavs back to "their own lands." Soon there would be no lingering reminders of the presence of the Slavic barbarians.

It didn't matter to Mussolini that the Venetians had needed them to populate the peninsula hundreds of years ago, after the plagues. For now there were Italians with no homes and no land. Mussolini needed their votes, their support, and the Slavs could go back to where they came from, or to hell itself, for all he cared.

Martin accepted the job in the commercial ship works in Novi Sad.

CHAPTER SEVEN

Starting over

It was the life Katarina had lived that she would miss, not the things in the house.

They sold — virtually gave, really — the house in Medulin to Martin's cousin. Leaving it empty would just open the door for the Italians to take it, and that would be insupportable. Maybe they could return and get it back some day. They had to hold out that hope.

Katarina nursed little Zora and thought about her life, about how she would grow up far away from all the things her mother held dear. What would that be like, to have a daughter who didn't know the home you grew up in, the family that had surrounded you, the hill you walked every day, the cemetery? What would it be like for Zora to be a stranger to this place that had been so dear to Marinovič and Rojnič for so many generations?

Katarina determined then that she would tell her stories, repeated often, so that Zora would feel as if she knew the place. She would know how her family got there. She would know how happy they had been for generations, for hundreds of years. She would know how unfair it was that it had been stolen from them for no reason. But Katarina would also teach Zora to be open to whatever life threw at her. The world was so complicated these days, and politicians drew maps anywhere they wanted. One shouldn't get too attached, that's what Katarina would teach her. It just leads to heartache.

The day of departure finally arrived. The night before, Katarina checked the things the girls had put aside to take with them before putting out her dress for the next day. The girls owned so little. They each had a few clothes to put in their pillowcases, along with a comb, a toy, an extra pair of shoes. The older girls each had a mirror.

And then they had to say goodbye to Bogdan and Roža.

"Listen, *brate*, brother, you can still come with us, you know." Martin couldn't just give up on them.

"You know I can't, Martin. Roža and I have discussed it endlessly. I can keep my job, and her whole family is here. Who would take care of her parents if we leave? We wish you all the best, Martin, but we will try to stay here, at least for now. I will write and tell you how it goes." His voice broke and he held his brother-in-law close, not knowing when they would meet again. He moved off to get Roža and young Matte so they could all say their goodbyes.

Katarina felt the tears flowing as she went back in the house, and wished once more that they, too, could stay. But it was too late to think about that. She went to bundle up Zora. *So young, so delicate, and already a refugee,* she thought as she packed a few more diapers.

Martin came in, finally admitting to himself that the others were staying put. It was just his way of saying goodbye, of assuring himself that he had done all he could for them. There was no right or wrong, no choice was good now, but he had to make the offer. It might be the last chance for a while.

It seemed the borders were closing, and all existing passports had been cancelled. Not that anyone other than Martin had a passport. What did they need one for?

He knew Zora's birth certificate said she was born in Italy. Would this new country to which Serbia now belonged recognize her? Would there even be a Serbia for long? It was all so complicated, the end of this war. They would be part of this new kingdom, this Yugoslavia. They would all be Slavs, hopefully living together in peace. It would be love-ly if they could live in peace for a time.

As the girls rushed around upstairs, Martin took a final look at the home in which he had spent his entire life. He could find every nick in the stone walls blindfolded, and had watched his father build most of the furniture. It was a strong building that had stood for hundreds of years and could survive that many more, but his daughters might never see the inside of it again. He knew that his relatives had wanted another home for their large family. This would be part of their compound, and he knew it was permanent. They were uncomfortably close to the government and the Italians, and they were as scornful of his decision to leave as he was disgusted with them for their compliance. But they acted as if everything was fine, and they were just doing his family a big favor.

He climbed the stairs to help Katarina, taking a final look at the bed in which he had been conceived and was born: where he had first been with Katarina and where his own children had been conceived. He needed to move on before it became unbearable.

The last ship was waiting for them in the old Na-vy harbor. Bogdan helped bundle everyone into the old cart and hurried the horse along the road. The harbor was eerily quiet, all of the other ships had gone.

The girls each had their own issues. Mara, the oldest, was sad and tense for she was leaving behind Matte, a young man she was secretly in love with. The others were too young to think about what they were leaving behind, but the melancholy mood slowly infected them. Martin finally got them all down to the small stateroom they would share for the next few days. As they got themselves organized, they could feel the motors increase their speed, and the ship started moving away from the dock.

"It's a good, strong ship," Martin said, although he hoped it was his last time on board a military ship. He was happy he had the job at the commercial ship building facility in Petrovaradin. They needed more ships for trading, not for fighting. He didn't want to build warships or work with any country's military ever again.

The ship pulled out of the port and Katarina realized she might never see her village again. She couldn't stop staring. As Medulin shrank behind them, she suddenly saw it from another point of view, as a stranger might. It was so small. What would bring her daughters back, once they had lived in the bigger world? Even if the Italians left some day, it would never be the same.

She knew, then, with finality, that after 400 years, it was over. Her daughters would live lives she had never imagined. They might marry men they hadn't grown up with. They would be part of a larger world.

And what would it be like for her to live far from the house that was built by her grandparents' grandparents? To cook in a kitchen where she or Martin hadn't eaten every meal of their lives? To sleep in a bed that had not held any of her seven newborn babies?

She pulled Zora close to her breast. "Your life will be far different from mine, little one. I don't know what lies ahead for you, but I do know you'll be surrounded by love."

Just then little Jana ran up. "Mama, Tata says you have to come down. Mara won't stop crying. She says she misses Matte too much to go on. And Slavića is crying too, because Mara is sad. And Roža looks like she's getting sick, Mama, but I'm not sad. I can't wait to see our new home. Tata says there is a river nearby, and he can go fishing just like he did before."

Katarina took one last look at the past, but really couldn't see much anymore. Only the church at the top of the hill was still visible, with the cemetery that she knew was next to it. Then Jana pulled her away into the confusion that was her brood of girls, that only she could calm, as she always had.

During the trip, Katarina thought about Medulin again and again. She knew she had to move forward. She had to stop worrying.

"I promise you, Katarina, we are going to a secure part of the country, and I know you will like our house there. I have a good job, and that is the most important thing," Martin kept telling her.

"Oh, Martin. How can I help but worry?" They had just fled one part of the country because Mussolini couldn't bear for anyone to be anything but Italian. Even without much access to news, she had heard about the fight between the Hungarians and the Serbs over their new home. They might encounter problems there, too. "Why can't we just go to the coast, or even Belgrade?"

"Katarina, Petrovaradin is a small, pretty town, right on the Danube. Give it a chance," Martin said. Besides, they had been worrying too long. It was time to just put their heads down and see what the future would bring.

The Hungarians wouldn't get that part of the country, he was sure of it. The Yugoslav government wouldn't set up the shipping there if they were worried.

He had heard that the King of Yugoslavia was a good man, and that the new union was powerful and growing. This time the Serbs had the right idea and would gather all the southern Slav countries together for a permanent, peaceful union.

Katarina was sure that Martin was not as confident as he sounded, but she knew he was right. There was no point in getting the girls all worried. She and Martin would have to act as if giving everything up and diving into the unknown was not a big issue, as if everything would be all right. For now, she had to get her girls organized for the rest of the trip. The Serbs, the Croats, the Bosnians, the Italians, the Hungarians — even the Russians — they would all have to argue it out without her.

.

CHAPTER EIGHT

Haven in Yugoslavia

Petrovaradin was every bit as comforting as Martin promised. Their years there proved good ones. Martin was happy with his job, and it felt secure. They had two more daughters, Milena and Ljuba. Martin greeted each as if he had never been luckier. The girls all grew up speaking Serbian, went to school, and never gave a thought to their parents' past, or to Istria.

Their oldest daughter Mara persisted with her childhood sweetheart Matte, writing him regularly and even finding a way to visit his family one time. The result was predictable, given her determination. They married, moved into the home Matte shared with his parents in Zagreb, the capital of Croatia, and soon had a son, Dragan.

In Petrovaradin, Katarina and Martin's second daughter, Roža, met and married a transplanted Bosnian, Ivan, and they moved into a small house nearby. They had two children, a boy and a girl, and now Roža was pregnant again, with her third.

But the outside world wasn't sitting still. While their lives moved smoothly along, politics in Europe started getting uncomfortable once again. Mussolini and the Fascists were growing increasingly more militant. Germany had a new leader, a little Austrian with a deranged-looking face and strange hair, who wanted to recreate an old empire . . . or invent a new one. Whatever it was, Yugoslavia, too, was getting nervous. The shipbuilding work Martin so enjoyed was shifting back to military work, and he wanted nothing to do with it.

And then it was 1938 and it all seemed to be starting again. The Hungarian fascists threatened the area around Novi Sad. Martin decided they had to leave. Katarina was reluctant, for she kept thinking one of those Hungarian soldiers could turn out to be her son. But deep inside she knew they had to move out of danger.

A family friend from Istria had settled in Zagreb, back in Croatia, and started a machine shop. He asked Martin to come join him and help develop business with other parts of the country. The possibility of working with an old friend and moving out of range of the Hungarian military finally convinced them to make the move to Zagreb. There, Katarina was closer to Mara and her family, but she missed Roža and her children, who had stayed behind. It seemed they might never all be together again.

Their daughter Slavića struggled with the shift. The oldest one still at home, she found a job, but never seemed as happy after the move. Zora and her other sisters, however, merged into the new environment quickly, focusing on school and adapting as if they had always lived in Croatia. At sixteen, Zora loved going to school, read whenever she could, and helped her mother in the kitchen and her sisters with their schoolwork.

"Zorića, you have to pay attention," Katarina said one day, not for the first time. "Get your head out of that book; Ljubica and Milena need help with their reading."

Katarina continued with her baking. All three of the younger girls were in the kitchen with their schoolbooks, as usual.

"Just one more minute, Mama. I promised the teacher I would return this book tomorrow. And I just haven't had time to read it." Zora barely looked up.

"I know, *sladka*, sweet one. I'm sorry," her mother continued. With Mara and Roža both gone she counted on Zora to carry more of the burden of helping her sisters.

It was late afternoon, and soon Slavića walked into the house and straight to the kitchen. She greeted them all, then turned to her mother. "Mama, I ran into the postman on my way home from work. There's a letter for you from Roža," she said, giving her mother a thin envelope.

"Oh, lovely. I can't wait to read it." Roža was almost at term with her third child.

Slavića nodded. "Mama, she wrote me a letter last week. She wanted to know if I would come help her with the younger children. She is not feeling as strong as she did with the first two."

Katarina's joyful look disappeared. "Oh my God! Why didn't she tell me?" She read the brief letter, then turned to Slavića.

"She didn't want to worry you, Mama. But she needs help."

"What do you want to do?" Katarina asked her daughter.

"Mama, I really want to go," said Slavića. "I miss Petrovaradin so much. And I really think Rožića needs me."

"Oh, *sladka*, Roža and Ivan's house is so small. Slavića, where would you sleep?"

"She told me they've arranged one large bed for all the children in the bedroom. She and Ivan have put a small bed in the kitchen for themselves. I would sleep in the large bed with the children."

"I don't know, Slavića. You're just beginning to get settled here in Zagreb. Don't you want to stay in your job?" Katarina could barely think about this possible move. And how could she let Slavića go?

"Oh, there's lots of time for that, Mama. And you know I love being with babies."

"I do know that," Katarina replied, thoughtful. Her mind moved to the challenges this would raise. "Zora, you would have less time for school as well, as I would need more help."

"That's all right, Mama," interjected Zora. "If Roža needs help, then of course Slavića needs to go."

"I can be ready to get on the train by the day after tomorrow!" Roža's letter had told Slavića that she really, really needed help.

"Slavića," her mother said, eyes narrowing, "my letter just says Roža would like you to come spend a little bit of time with her. You're talking about leaving immediately. What are you not telling me?"

"Let me see it, Mama." Slavića read the letter her sister had written to their mother. It did sound as if Roža was just inviting her for a visit.

"Mama, you need to read the letter she wrote me. You have to know. She's not doing well."

"Oh dear." Tears started running down Katarina's face as she read the letter Slavića gave her. She had lost babies of her own. She knew how frightening labor and birth could be. And because Petrovaradin was still just a small town, the hospital stood across the Danube in Novi Sad.

"Of course you have to go right away." She couldn't protect Slavića, even though she had worried about her from the day she was conceived, in the dreadful circumstances of the last war. But she wouldn't think about that now. It had been so long ago and they had moved on. Now the girls were becoming adults and would all just have to work things out for themselves.

"But, Mama, I hate to leave you alone with all the young ones."

"They'll just all have to grow up a little faster. Life has a way of doing that to us, it seems."

"Oh, Zorića is growing up fast enough!" exclaimed Jana, who had walked in during this last conversation. "That tall handsome boy down the street from us has been hanging around an awful lot lately."

"What tall handsome boy?" Zora blushed as she said it, giving herself away. At sixteen she had developed into a beautiful young lady, and the young men were already noticing.

"Oh yes, I know, there are so many tall handsome boys," Jana teased. "You just can't keep track of them all."

The tension in the room eased, as it always did when Jana entered.

"Jana," said Katarina, "it looks like Slavića is going to have to go to Petrovaradin to help Roža with the birth."

"Oh dear! So things are not improving?" Jana turned to her sister as she said this.

"You mean you knew about it also?" asked Katarina.

"Yes, Mama," said Jana. "I knew they didn't want to worry you. But how lovely that Slavića will be able to go help. She's so good with babies. You know she will take good care of Roža and the babies."

"Maybe I do worry too much. It's probably because Martin is gone so often, and I can't get him out of my mind. It will be nice when he sets up his work to be closer to home."

However, Jana clearly had something else on her mind, and she needed to share it.

"Mama, there's one other thing we need to talk about." Jana was not so bubbly this time.

"Now you sound serious, *draga*."

"Oh, it's not something bad. In fact, it's very good! It's just hard to talk about something happy with Roža suffering."

"But what is it Jana?"

"Well," Jana paused, smiling in spite of herself. "Atza has asked me to marry him!"

"How exciting!" exclaimed Zora. "And you said he was just a friend."

"Well, he was at first. But when we were apart, after our family moved to Zagreb, Atza and I realized we really missed each other. He's been writing me every day!"

"We know; we've seen the letters," piped in little Milena.

"But he's not in Petrovaradin anymore, is he?" asked Katarina.

"Do you love him? Enough to move and leave us all?" interjected Zora.

"One at a time, one at a time," said Jana. "I love him, I want to marry him, and I hate to leave you, but Atza is who I want to be with for the rest of my life."

"*Bože moj*! Oh my God!" bemoaned Katarina. "I can't believe you're all scattering. My babies are leaving the nest."

"But where will you live?" Zora went back to questioning. She wanted the details.

"That's why he's asking now. He has a new job in Belgrade. He has an apartment, and he can support me while I look for work. He wants me to come see it."

"But that's wonderful," said Slavića. "We could go to Belgrade together. I could see your new apartment. Novi Sad is just seventy kilometers further. This will all work out after all."

The two of them went off, chattering and planning. Zora returned to her book, forgetting she was supposed to help Ljuba and Milena. And Katarina just wished Martin was home, so they could discuss these issues. She knew they were significant, but the girls seemed content, and she didn't want to concern them.

She was also very happy for Jana. She and Atza had been sweethearts for some time, and Katarina knew it was hard on Jana when they had moved away from Petrovaradin.

When Martin returned, he and Katarina talked about all the news. As they discussed Slavića's return to Petrovaradin, it became clear this was not the end of the bad news. Martin had heard from Istria, and it was grim. The shipyards at Pula had been reopened and there was much activity building warships. Mussolini and the Italians were belligerent. It seemed more and more these days that World War I — the so-called "war to end all wars" — had ended nothing. Slavića had been born from that war, and had helped heal her mother after it ended.

Was the nightmare to start again?

Zora and sisters circa 1930. Zora is the first from the right.
Probably in Petrovaradin, Vojvodina

CHAPTER NINE

World War II

Katarina's worst fears were realized with the advent of the second World War. Her family, like the whole country of Yugoslavia, was torn apart. Katarina, Martin, and the younger girls — along with their eldest daughter Mara's family — were living in Zagreb, the capital of Croatia. Slavića was now with Roža's family in Novi Sad, the capital of Vojvodina. Jana was in Belgrade, the capital of Serbia.

The country was split into pieces again. For Martin and Katarina, there could be no winner in this conflict.

Politically, Yugoslavia was a mess before the war even started. The nominal head of state was the Serbian regent, Prince Paul of Yugoslavia, with a Prime Minister serving in Belgrade. In Croatia, meanwhile, separatists continuously fought to establish greater autonomy.

The Yugoslavian central government, already weak and fearing defeat at the hands of the Axis powers, finally negotiated a Pact with the Germans to avoid senseless fighting. They chose subjection over war.

But the Serbian people would have none of this. They rose in protest and staged a coup against the government. They would not collaborate with the Nazis and the Fascists — no matter how high the cost. And the cost was unbearably high. The action that followed was swift and brutal. The Germans launched a full-scale attack on Serbia.

It started on April 6, 1941 and was over in eleven days — only eleven days to destroy a country, but a very important eleven days for the world.

Hitler, outraged that Serbia dared defy him, decided to destroy the upstart country. The Germans staged a massive air attack on Belgrade, and their land forces came in from Bulgaria, Romania and Austria. The Hungarians drove through Vojvodina. The Italian army attacked through Ljubljana in Slovenia and from Italian Istria along the Dalmatian coast.

To do this Hitler had to postpone his long planned invasion of Russia by four weeks — the most important four-week delay of the entire war.

The invasion of the Soviet Union by Germany — the largest military invasion in the history of warfare — therefore didn't start until June 22, 1941, postponed by one month from the original detailed plans. As a result of that delay, in early December German troops, believed to be within four weeks of a final victory, were crippled by an unexpectedly deep Russian winter. Hitler's troops were just outside Moscow. Instead of victory, it was the beginning of the end for Germany.

Serbia's defiance and refusal to collaborate had made all the difference, but Serbia paid a high price. Central Serbia was occupied by the Germans as an enemy state. Vojvodina was annexed to Hungary.

Croatia, where the family was living, took the opposite path. They refused to fight the Germans and Italians, and on April 10, 1941 — led by the *Ustaše* under the right-wing radical government of Ante Pavelič — became the Independent State of Croatia, a puppet state of the Germans. The *Ustaše* were violent in their hatred of Serbs, and followed the Nazi tenets of anti-Semitism. By this point in time, however, the family had no alternatives and remained in Zagreb.

The populations of all the countries were subject to random and horrific atrocities that led to enormous numbers of deaths. Even though the official fighting was over almost before it began, the hard days of hunger and quotas and waiting in lines and secret battles had just started. The Marinovič family, like so many, was split in three different war zones. They were on opposite sides of the war in what were suddenly different countries speaking different languages. As they could not communicate with each other, Katarina could only hope her daughters and their families were safe.

Slavića, in Petrovaradin to care for Roža, had grown to love the two children, and took care of Roža's husband Ivan as well while Roža was in the hospital in nearby Novi Sad. But Roža died in childbirth and Slavića stayed on to take care of the new baby and help the family, now with three children under five years of age. One thing led to another, and after a year Ivan asked her to stay. While the whole region was annexed by Hungary, Petrovaradin was small enough to be left mostly alone, and Slavića's new family—for she soon married Ivan—could grow most of the food they needed. She felt sheltered in their tiny house and was too busy with babies to think about the war.

The central neighborhood of Belgrade where Jana and her husband lived with their baby during the war was heavily bombed. Three days of massive attacks — with no declaration of war and no warning to the civilian population — destroyed much of the city center, including the war ministry, the post office, telegraph and power stations. Up to twenty percent of the housing was destroyed.

The terror of those days and nights was unimaginable. A building next to Jana's apartment house collapsed, and fires raged everywhere, but their building was spared. Fortunately, their apartment remained usable and eventually the city was rebuilt around them. But food and power were hard to come by, and transportation networks were destroyed.

Meanwhile, Martin and Katarina kept their heads down in Zagreb. Devastated that their own part of the country had submitted to the Nazis without resistance, they couldn't believe it was their own countrymen, now led by a Nazi sympathizer, who persecuted Serbs — including neighbors and acquaintances.

Their small apartment was on a busy central street in the city, with a tramway down the middle that Martin used to get to work. Although the city was not bombed until the end of the war, life was a constant battle to find enough food, and they had to queue up for hours every day.

"Martin, I am worried to death about our missing girls," lamented Katarina one day in the midst of the war. It was a Saturday and Zora had taken her younger sisters to the market where farmers brought vegetables, hoping to find something for their dinner. "You know the Serbs are suffering even more than we are. I wish there was some way to find out how they are."

"And we haven't heard from my brother or any of the family in Istria for years," she continued. "The last war tore us up, but this feels almost worse. It feels like it might never end."

"You're right, Katarina. Not knowing what is happening to them is impossible." Martin was always telling the girls that the war would soon be over, but he really wasn't sure how long it would go on. "Thank God I got out of military work when I did," he continued. "I don't know who I would be working for if I hadn't. Pavlič has the schools teaching in German now. And they are being taught the evil and hatred that his party is spreading. I thought the Italians were bad, but this is worse."

"Yes, but you know the girls don't believe any of that. Most of the people don't, thank goodness. I couldn't live knowing they were all animals." Katarina instinctively moved to put the *jezva,* the tall Turkish style coffee pot, on the fire, as she always did when they needed distraction, but then remembered that there was no more coffee and only enough gas for a quick meal. She studied her husband's crestfallen expression. She knew he was remembering the last war, and how its result forced them into this movement between countries. She, too, still felt rootless and stateless.

At least they were still speaking Croatian at home. Whenever things got tough, they remembered how their language was outlawed before that earlier exile. It was a key symbol of repression to them, the banning of the language. It was also all they had left that remained consistent in their lives.

"Well, it's not the first time that German is the language of our home, you know," Katarina continued, remembering, trying to reassure him — or perhaps herself. "The birth records at the church in Medulin were in a Germanic language even when my grandmother was born, while it was part of Austro-Hungary."

"That's true, but the Austrian Empire didn't try to convert us all into German speakers. We kept our language for centuries. I'm not so sure what these Germans will do now. And our own countrymen are persecuting Serbs. Its hard to tell who's the enemy."

"But Martin, our daughters in Serbia are much worse off," Katarina continued, rubbing a *jezva* that didn't need more burnishing. She knew Belgrade had been bombed and that the Germans were killing Serbs in reprisal for choosing the wrong side of the war. She was frightened and torn by conflicting emotions. "It's not the Serbs; it's us. We Croats are on the wrong side of this war as far as I'm concerned . . . but at least we aren't being bombed. I worry about Jana. I know Atza will fight the Germans any way he can."

"*Duše*, you're right. But none of us have alternatives now. We can't go back there, and they can't come here." They also couldn't go home to Istria, for things were not any better there. Martin had secretly hoped for a time that they could return to their little town of Medulin, but they no longer owned a home there, and it was close to Pula. With the giant military shipyards there, it was even more dangerous. "We have to stay here for now."

"And there's still that *prokleti* Mussolini," growled Katarina. "He's been a curse on our existence since Zora was born. Now he's teamed up with Hitler."

Martin interrupted, now the one trying to calm things down. "You know, Katarina, you have to stop that now. We're under the Germans, and the Italians are their allies. You never know who is on their side. Please don't say any more about Mussolini or Hitler. It's really dangerous. I don't want the girls to start talking carelessly."

The door opened and Zora came in with some beets and potatoes in the string bag she always carried. Soon the kitchen was bustling with girls, and talk of problems was forgotten. Throughout these tough times Zora steadfastly refused to get involved in politics. She had a job in the city, in an office. It was boring, but kept her distracted and helped pay for food when it was available. If she had private dreams, she kept them to herself and focused her energy on her sisters and parents and on just getting through this time.

Zora was never one to talk loosely. She had been horrified when she began really understanding what her countrymen were doing. How could they side with those evil Fascists and Nazis? When the war ended, which had to be soon, she knew she would have to find a way to create meaning to her life. And it would not be with one of these toadying *Ustaše*, no matter how blond and handsome they might be. She would find her own way no matter how long that took.

CHAPTER TEN

Zora finds her way

By the time it was over, more than one million people died in Yugoslavia during the Second World War.

Seventeen when it started, Zora became an adult during the war. Surrounded by the enemy, she just kept her head down. Her protests were mostly silent, or in discussions with close friends. They managed to turn the phrase "Heil Hitler" into a sarcastic curse in their language, but participated in no active rebellion.

The sisters and their families were out of touch with each other for much of the duration, but when they finally all reconnected, they were relieved to learn that everyone had survived. Slowly, they once again picked up their lives and moved on.

By 1943, the resistance movement was spreading throughout the country, and two years later the fighting was over, the Germans defeated. In the end, the Partisan resistance, mostly Serbs, joined with the Communists under the Croatian-born leader Marshall Josip Broz Tito, to help the United States and its allies drive the Germans out of the country in 1945. More deaths followed as accused collaborators from all the republics were killed in retribution, along with many innocent people.

When it was over, a new Yugoslavia was formed. Six fairly independent republics—Serbia, Croatia, Slovenia, Macedonia, Bosnia and Montenegro—were united under one government. Kosovo and Vojvodina were named autonomous provinces under the Republic of Serbia. Thus emerged the new Communist country, the Socialist Federative Republic of Yugoslavia.

The new capital was Belgrade, in Serbia. By law Serbia was an equal republic to Croatia and the others. But many Croatians were outraged with the outcome. The Nazis were defeated, but the leadership was back in Serbia. Many Croats, mostly *Ustaše,* left the country to agitate through an international terrorist movement for separation. They would continue that agitation for years.

Although Martin and Katarina lived in Zagreb, the capital of Croatia, they had never identified with the separatist Croatians or the *Ustaše.* They were relieved to have the family safe under one flag. They favored the union and wanted Yugoslavia to go forward as one country. Their great concern now was the return of Istria from the Italians.

For Zora, all opportunity for further education had dissolved with the war. Transition from schoolgirl to a significant contributor to the family finances had been the only option. She had always kept her dreams of advanced studies in mathematics a secret, but now that it was over she wanted to find work more challenging than her clerical assignments.

The population of Yugoslavia celebrated the end of the war and young people, especially, tried to forget those years of hardship and focus on moving forward. Zora knew she wanted more out of life. But it wasn't always easy to balance a desire for a challenging position with wanting a carefree existence, especially with fear no longer hanging over their heads.

Vibrant, petite and attractive, now in her early twenties, Zora had plenty of admirers. Her dark hair and eyes complemented her smooth creamy skin. In spite of ongoing shortages, she always looked classy. She had learned to sew her own clothes, carefully following newsreels to see the latest styles, as much as for the news. She was thrilled when she could replace the heavy walking shoes of the war with a pair of handmade leather slippers with a nice heel.

She wanted a large family like the one she grew up in, but was in no hurry to start. Handsome men would show up regularly to take her to a café or out dancing. Her sisters teased her about one particular blond fellow who seemed to hover protectively, but she insisted she preferred taller men, and dark hair.

The country's leadership, meanwhile, was working to reconstruct the economy after the war and move forward technologically. National services, starting with energy and telecommunications, were being reestablished.

One evening, a year or so after the war's end, Katarina was preparing dinner in the kitchen of their small apartment near the heart of Zagreb when Zora came home from her job. Martin was back from work and sat at the table, as he often did, smoking one of his handmade cigarettes and talking. He looked up and smiled at his daughter, who looked particularly beautiful in a stylish dark blue wool dress that dropped just below the knee.

"Mama, Tata, I have a new job." She could hardly contain herself, needing to tell them all about it. She quickly pulled off her hat and jacket, and filled a glass with water as she prepared to launch into her planned conversation.

"What kind of job?" Martin looked at her questioningly.

"It's very exciting. My friend's father works as a manager in the telecommunications headquarters, and he introduced me to the head of the switchboard operators." Here she paused as if announcing a news headline.

"I will be a long distance operator."

The silence grew. She was about to fill it when her mother finally said, "But Zora, we don't even have a telephone. What do you know about long distance switchboards?"

Zora laughed. She knew her mother didn't understand her love of mathematics and technical things. Mama was from a different generation, a different world. But Zora had waited a long time for this opportunity. The new systems were now being installed all over the country. This, she believed, was the technology that was going to change the world. She was going to be in on the beginning.

"Oh, Mama, I don't need to know anything; I will be learning on the job. But they gave me a test and they said I passed with great results. You know I love using my mind that way. And besides," she added, jumping up in her excitement, "soon we will have a phone."

"Really?" Now it was her father's turn. This was the first Martin had heard of it. None of their neighbors had a phone. "Why would we need one?"

"Well. The office has to be able to reach me in case of an emergency. We will be moved to the top of the list as soon as I've finished my first, probationary, month."

"Are you sure we should have a phone in the house? Are they safe? I've heard they let off some kind of fumes," said Katarina.

"Oh, those are old wives' tales, Mama. Phones are completely safe; they've been around for a long time." Zora knew that their country needed to progress after all the chaos with the war. The new Communist government was pushing for these advances.

"Aren't you thinking about going back to school, going to university, Zora? You had hoped to do that before the war." Katarina remembered Zora's ambitions from years ago.

"No, Mama," Zora shook her head dismissively. "I am too old for that. Besides, I think I can learn just as much and make progress while I am working. That way I can earn a living at the same time."

"Please, Zora," interjected her father, "be careful you don't push too hard. You know the *vlasti* — the powers — won't let you advance too far if you aren't in the party." When someone said *vlasti*, it was known that it was the Communist party they meant. Zora knew her father feared the Communists and didn't want to be too closely linked to them. He no longer trusted government of any kind and wanted nothing more than a low profile for his family. Zora had thought this through carefully. She knew that party membership was both a way to succeed and something to be cautious of. She had no intention of joining, but believed she could do well anyway.

"Tata, I am so tired of thinking about what the *vlasti* will or will not allow. During the war it was the Germans, now it's the Communists or the government in Belgrade. I am just going to do a great job and think about what is possible rather than what is not allowed. I'm tired of all that. I'm not just a little mouse waiting to be stepped on!"

She regretted her words the minute she said them. Her parents had been through a lot and she didn't want to seem critical, or dismissive of their fears. But it was a new world, and she wanted to be part of it. Her father, however, surprised her.

"You're right, *duša*," said Martin, nodding his head, as if at an old memory and smiling. He was remembering himself, as a young man, leaving Istria rather than being walked all over by Mussolini. "You're young, and you see your life in front of you. I have seen too many things fall apart in my life. I'll just have to try to look at the world through your eyes." But it was hard for him to keep from worrying about life going out of their control. It had happened so often before.

"Thank you, Tata. Have faith in me."

"Will you be working for the government?"

"Yes. Well, for the Postal and Telegraph Service, but that is part of the government."

"Does that mean you have to join the Communist Party?"

Martin really couldn't let go of his discomfort. He had no love for Marshall Tito and his links to the Soviet Union. He was tired of politics, and war, and all the turbulence.

"No, Tata, I don't." Zora was about to continue when the door burst open and her sisters Milena and Ljuba walked in. The two of them couldn't have been more different. At twenty, Milena had the dark Marinovič hair and eyes, but she was short and plump and soft, with a ready smile and always something funny, yet biting, to say. She had never had any ambitions beyond marriage and children. Ljuba was her opposite in every way. All edges and angles, her appearance was defined as much by her glasses as by the briefcase she carried with her everywhere. Although only eighteen, she was the most ambitious of the girls. Her clothes were no-nonsense, and she didn't give them any thought, happy when Zora offered to sew something for her.

Ljuba was the one, they all knew, who would be able to take advantage of this new world that was emerging after the war. The youngest daughter, she was finishing secondary school, and had always just assumed she would continue on to University. She wanted to work in the advanced medical research lab that was one of Zagreb's most prestigious institutions.

"Why are you home so early, Zora?" asked Milena, who clearly hadn't expected to see her.

"I have a new job at the telephone exchange," exclaimed Zora.

"What will you be doing?" asked Ljuba. She shared Zora's passion for mathematics and science. Zora had always helped her with her schoolwork until it became clear Ljuba no longer needed any help and was, in fact, surpassing her tutor in knowledge. By now Zora knew she would never catch up with her little sister. But she was determined to progress in her own way.

"Well," she replied, "I will be working on the main switchboard for the whole country."

"Does that mean all phone calls will go through you?" asked Ljuba.

Most homes in Yugoslavia didn't have telephones yet, and calling a foreign country was exotic. People just wrote letters. A phone call could be made from the central headquarters, but it was prohibitively expensive.

"No. With today's technology, most local calls are connected directly. Only long distance calls go through the switchboard. We are already connected to almost all the countries in the world."

"Which countries will you work with?" asked Ljuba, clearly excited about this new opportunity for Zora. She dreamed of going to England to study some day. Having a sister in the telecommunications hub of the country could be an asset.

"Well, I will be responsible for the calls to Belgrade, where they can be redirected to the rest of the country." It was a very important connection, especially since all the Yugoslav government offices were in Belgrade.

"So will you be able to talk to Slavića and Jana?" asked Milena, the link to family igniting a little interest.

"No, they don't have phones yet, either. I will mostly be talking to people who are working on the exchange. Maybe to some in businesses or government agencies. I'll know more after I start."

"When is that?" asked Katarina.

"Well, I told them I would be available in two weeks. I already resigned at the office, and they told me I could leave at the end of the week."

"That's exciting, Zora. I wish I knew someone who could help me get a job like that," said Milena, with a smile. But her mind seemed elsewhere.

"You know that's not true, Milena," exclaimed Zora. Milena had been seeing Dule, a colleague, for some time already. "You want to get married and have babies, not have a career!"

"That is true, and . . ." Milena didn't get to finish before Ljuba interrupted, wanting to learn more about Zora's new job.

"But, Zora, you speak Hungarian and a bit of Italian. Won't you get to work in the foreign section?"

"Maybe later, Ljuba. Right now I need to get trained. Besides, I like the idea of starting with Belgrade, where everything is based. I might be able to visit the headquarters there. Then I could see our Jana and her children."

"Will you be working at the large building downtown?"

"Yes, the telephone exchange is on the second floor. It's one of the historic buildings of Zagreb, you know," said Zora.

"But Zora," interjected Martin, "that building was bombed during the war. Has that all been repaired? Is it safe?"

"It's not just repaired, Tata; it's been extensively modernized." She knew they had some of the newest technologies in the country because of the reconstruction work that had been done. "They redesigned the whole second floor around the new long distance and international capabilities."

"Now, you're sure about this Communist Party thing?" Martin just couldn't stop worrying about it.

"Oh yes, Tata. My friend's father has a very good job there, and he told me he is not a party member."

Zora didn't tell her father that the man had also suggested she keep her head down and not get involved in political debates on the job.

"And can they use the phone line to listen in on us when we get a phone?" Katarina asked.

"Mama, I don't think anyone wants to hear what we talk about. Especially if it's Milena talking to Dule. Just think, Milena, you wouldn't have to worry about where to meet him, you could just call."

"Well, that would be nice if they had a phone at his apartment," said Milena, finally getting their attention. "Listen, everyone, this is great news from Zora, but I have good news, too.

"Dule has proposed!" Milena almost shouted in her excitement.

"*Pa to je divno*! But that's wonderful!" Katarina leaped up and wrapped Milena in a big hug.

"And did you accept?" Ljuba teased.

"I didn't have to. He knew my answer."

"When is the big day?"

"Very soon. Dule's mother can't wait for us all to live together. She will move out of the bedroom and will have an alcove in the living room. So we can all stay in their apartment; it's a good location, really close by." The plan also neatly solved the problems with housing shortages rampant in the country. There were waiting lists, and they were particularly long in the cities.

"That's wonderful, *draga*," Katarina was already walking toward the kitchen. "Bring him over to-night. We'll celebrate over my *sarme*. You know how much he loves them."

"We all love your *sarme*," said Martin. Katarina's *sarme* were a unique take on the dish that wrapped meat and rice in cabbage. She brined her cabbage, so it was a bit tart, halfway to sauerkraut. It was some-thing she had learned from a Hungarian neighbor when they lived in Petrovaradin.

Martin too, hugged Milena. "I can't wait to con-gratulate the lucky man who is getting my beautiful daughter. Make some extra *sarme*, Katarina; I've worked up an appetite just thinking about them."

Zora wiped a tear from her eye as they all hugged. She was embarrassed at how easily she teared up, her emotions showing. But these were tears of joy for her sister and for her own step into her future.

"Are you upset, Zora?" asked her sister, misunderstanding her emotions.

"No, Milena, I am thrilled. Why would I be upset?"

"Well, you are older, and I thought you might wish to be married first. Not that you seem short of suitors."

"Oh, Milena, they are just friends."

"You always say that, but I'm not sure that's all they want to be. They are always hanging around you," teased Ljuba.

"I'm not ready to get married yet," declared Zora. "I want to start my career and see some other places before I settle down."

"You always did know your own mind. I should have realized you wouldn't mind." Milena smiled as they hugged again.

"You've always known what you wanted, too, Milena. And now you have it."

Milena went off to invite Dule to dinner, Ljuba returned to her schoolwork. Zora went into the kitchen to join her mother in cooking the *sarme*. Zora was already a good cook. She had grown up in her mother's kitchen, after all. She started chopping the onions, and Katarina prepared the cabbage leaves.

"Be sure you chop them really fine," said Katarina. "You know your father doesn't like it when he can taste the onions."

"I know, I know, Mama. How many times have I watched you do it?"

"Hundreds, I suppose. You always liked spending time in the kitchen when you were younger. Maybe you'll run a restaurant some day."

"I don't think so. But I do like baking *torte*, cakes. Should I make one for the lovebirds?"

"That's a great idea. We have some fresh eggs. I think there are eight."

"Great. We can make your usual *krem torta*, cream cake, for eight." It was the simplest *torta*, three layers with a rich cream in between—chocolate when there was cocoa—but it was a tradition in the family to have it whenever eggs were available and there was something to celebrate. It required one egg for each serving, and the eggs had to be separated. Zora got to work on the *torta*, the two of them talking the whole time.

"Zorića, I have an idea for you," her mother said, without pausing in her work.

"Yes?" Zora said, turning to look at her mother.

Katarina hesitated. "I'd like to go home, to Istria, to visit Medulin," she said at last.

Zora almost broke the egg yolk she was removing. She kept her voice even, trying not to show her surprise. "When?"

"Well, you have some time before you have to start working; what about now?"

"Now?" Zora had never traveled anywhere with her mother. The subject had never even come up. She knew all about Medulin, but it was foreign—part of Italy. They never talked about going there. "But does Tata have time? And would he go?"

"You know he wouldn't go. He hated the Italians and the takeover of our home more than even I did. He swore he wouldn't go back until it was our soil again."

"Well, it might be our soil again soon. Now that the Italians sided with the Germans in the war and lost, they say it will be taken away from them."

"But I don't want to wait. I'd like to see my brother again. I want to swim in *my* sea, walk down *my* street, talk to the ones who were able to stay. I'd like it if the two of us could go."

"Did you just come up with this idea, Mama?" Zora was caught off guard.

"No, I've talked to Martin about it in principle, but he won't change his mind about going. And besides, he's busy with this new job."

"He's always busy with a new job." Zora paused, frowning slightly. "But why do you want to go now?"

"I just want to go back before I get too old," said her mother, avoiding meeting Zora's eyes. "And your new job gives us an opportunity."

"Mama, I know how much you have always hated it that you had to leave your home. Are you thinking of going back to live there?" Something about this nagged at Zora.

"No, *sladka*, sweetie; that time is long past. I admit I dreamed about nothing else for years. But we're older now, and all of you are settled here. What would your father and I do by ourselves there? Besides, it still isn't part of our country, although it's looking more like it will be soon."

"Mama, did you ever regret leaving?"

"No, dear, I didn't. I couldn't bear the thought of Martin suffering every day at the hands of the Italians and being forced to give up our language. And I knew I could never feel secure there, so close to the border." Zora had never heard Katarina talk about her experiences during the First World War, when she was forced to go out of the country, to Hungary.

Zora didn't know that even now, after all these years, her mother could barely stand thinking about it. She had lost her sons. She had been physically

violated. She had lived for months in near permanent terror. She had felt more helpless and heartbroken than she would ever feel again. And she still
resolved never to speak of it, even with her daughter, so Zora knew nothing about those years.

"Do you?" Katarina suddenly asked.

"Do I regret it that you left Istria?" asked Zora,
surprised.

"Yes, do you regret that we had to move around
the country? That your sisters are scattered, that we
got caught up in the Croatian separatist situation . . ."

"Oh, Mama," Zora interrupted. "That is over. I
don't think about politics. I am happy to be in Zagreb—it's such a beautiful city. My friends are here,
my new job, my whole life. I never even think about
Istria," Zora continued. "But now that you've suggested it, I am excited about going to visit my birthplace. I don't remember it at all."

"Well, let's go as soon as possible," said Katarina,
putting down her spoon. She seemed ready to go
immediately. "I have saved enough for the trip, and
we can stay with family when we arrive."

"Would it just be the two of us? I'd really like
that, Mama," said Zora.

"I think so. Ljuba can't miss school, and Milena
will be all wrapped up in her wedding plans."

"That would be lovely. With so many of us in the household, I have never had you to myself for a whole week!" Zora smiled hugely, excited at this new opportunity. She loved her mother, but always had to share her.

"I know, *sladka moja,* my sweet one. Let me tell your father before you talk to anyone else about it, all right?"

"Sure," Zora said, caught off guard yet again. "Doesn't he know?"

"Well, I haven't exactly told him I will go without him." Katarina paused, as if she had just remembered how all this started. She reached out and hugged Zora. "I really am very excited about your new job. It will be overshadowed, I'm afraid, by Milena's marriage. But I am so happy for you."

"Thanks, Mama." Zora wrapped her arms around her mother. "I am so pleased for Milena. She deserves her happiness. And now, on top of my new job, I have this trip to look forward to."

"Are you sure you don't mind that Milena is getting married first?"

"No, Mama, I don't," said Zora. She and Ljuba were the only two in the family who wanted anything more out of life than just marriage and a family. "You know the last two men I was seeing wanted me to marry them. But I am not ready, and they weren't the right ones, even though Tata really liked that handsome Croat. If I give up my freedom, it will have to be worth it!"

"You always did value your independence." Her mother laughed, as if to herself.

"I just don't want to be tied down yet. Besides," Zora smiled, "when I get married, I want lots of babies. Their father will have to be pretty wonderful."

"I'm quite sure anyone you pick will be unique. Now put those pans in the oven and go work with Ljuba a bit. She still likes it when you sit with her."

Zora had poured the batter for the *torte* layers into the three ancient black pans, having first rubbed a bit of lard on the bottom and sides so the cake could rise a bit. She now checked that the temperature was hot enough, and carefully put them into the oven.

As she walked out of the aromatic kitchen, Zora couldn't help but smile to herself, thinking about traveling with her mother. They had never actually taken a trip anywhere. If they traveled it was because they were moving somewhere because her father had to change jobs. She adored her mother; they all did. Someday she wanted to be just like her. She might like having some sons, as well as daughters, but she always saw her future in a warm kitchen with children all around.

She acted as if she didn't care about getting married, and she didn't mind that Milena had found someone first. She knew she had to wait for the right person. Oh, Dule was all right, but really, he was besotted with Milena. Zora wanted someone with a bit more backbone. That was the real issue with all her so-called admirers. She didn't want someone she could push around and always get her way with. Somehow, there had to be more to it if she was giving up her freedom.

She was sure the right person would come along someday. But right now she wanted to focus on the new job and, first, think about the upcoming trip with her mother. She couldn't wait to tell Ljuba.

That night Katarina talked to Martin about going to Istria with Zora. They had discussed it generally, but now she had a specific plan. They talked quietly, for the apartment was small, and the girls were in the next room.

"Katarina, are you sure about this trip?"

"Yes, Martin. I need to see it all one more time."

"But are you strong enough?" he asked, knowing the truth that hadn't been mentioned. It had been some time since the doctor had diagnosed breast cancer. But just as Katarina never talked about the horrible things that had happened when she was deported during the first world war, she would not talk about this. She wanted to enjoy her family as long as she could, and didn't want them treating her like an invalid. She felt fine. It was a small lump in her chest that had led to the diagnosis, and not debilitating pain.

"Yes, I know I can do it. Don't worry, Martin."

"Did you tell Zora what the doctor said?"

"Not yet," replied Katarina. "There will be time later. I want Zora to know where she came from. She was the last one born in Istria but she was so young when we left, she can't possibly remember anything."

"I will worry the whole time you are gone." Martin paced the small space around their bed. He wanted to hold her, but knew she would silence him with a caress.

"Please don't say that, Martin. You have been gone so often and for so long, I would've had a nervous breakdown if I worried every time. I can take care of myself, and Zora will be with me if I get worn out."

"Of course, I am worried." He was terrified, if the truth were told. Who would he be without her? But he wouldn't burden her with his nightmares. "I also know you have to do this. You have missed Medulin your whole life. No matter where we lived, no matter how good a face you put on things, I know you missed it, and that it was always home to you." He sat down on the bed, but faced away from her. He was afraid she would see the pain in his eyes if he looked at her.

"Let me do this trip and see, Martin, and then if we need to, we will talk to them all about it."

"Just promise me, *duse,* that you won't try and do too much or get too tired," he turned and put her head to his chest, needing to touch her.

"The doctor gave me hormone pills to take, the British think it could help. It could work, you know."

"They are apparently doing more study on those very drugs at the research center where Ljuba wants to work." Martin paused and smiled. "If only she would hurry, she might discover a cure."

"Oh, Martin, I am so glad you are keeping your sense of humor. Promise me you won't get too sad about this. Let's just live as if everything was normal." And she pulled him into the small bed they shared, grateful for the intimacy. His body was still strong, and she cherished the feel of him against her, which she knew deeply, whether he was close by or somewhere far away. His hair was grey, he had put on some weight since the days when he walked two hours to work every day, but his gentle eyes still softened when he looked at her or the girls, and he was still her Martin.

She really did love this stubborn man. How lucky she was he grew up right across the road from her. She and Martin had known each other all their lives, and still loved each other. Oh, it wasn't the hot romance girls expected today. But still. And he so loved the girls. He never let regrets — over the fate of his sons, the two wars, the exile, Roža's death, an entire life of challenges — take away from caring about her and their daughters. He was the only man she knew who just kept going, as if his life were always full of blessings. The girls would help him after she was gone, she knew.

"You know I never get sentimental," he said gently. "But just to make sure you miss me maybe I could spoil you a little . . ." he started.

"What do you want to do for me?"

"Well, maybe I'll learn to make the coffee . . ."

"All right, you can start in the morning." Katarina laughed. Martin had never stepped into a kitchen to do anything but have coffee, eat, drink, or talk.

"Well, let's not rush into anything."

Martin put his arms around Katarina and drew her close. He could feel her heart beating loudly. She was a lot more emotional about this than she let on, but he would let her take the lead. She had supported him in everything he needed to have his life run smoothly through all the trials of the past. Now it was his turn to give her as much room as she needed.

CHAPTER ELEVEN

Visiting
their homeland

A few days later Zora and her mother were on trains and buses headed to Medulin. A lifetime away in terms of their history, but only a few hours travel. There were still soldiers in the train stations, but the land in the center of the country was green and lush. As they reached the coast, it got drier and more rocky, but the glitter of the water hit Zora unexpectedly. She had lived by the Danube, but nothing had prepared her for the beauty of the Adriatic. They could see islands off in the distance and then suddenly they were approaching Rijeka and the atmosphere turned heavy.

When they changed trains in Rijeka they could see the damage caused by the war. The oil refineries and shipyard had been destroyed and the bombing was widespread. The city was still disputed between Yugoslavia and Italy, and lagged Zagreb greatly in recovery. But as soon as they left the city, they were back in comfortingly rural farmlands, with towns dotting the hilltops and reaching the water along the coast.

Her mother seemed somehow re-energized when they reached Pula, where Martin had worked at the shipyard. Katarina was back at home, but for Zora it was incredibly exotic. The city was built on seven hills overlooking the harbor, and had a beautiful natural setting. But that wasn't what captured her imagination. It was everything about it that was foreign. Zora felt as if she entered a new world. The Romans had built this city, and their traces could be seen everywhere. It was all on a vast scale. A two-thousand-year-old arena dominated the city, looking like a huge open-air museum. The enormous pillared Temple of Augustus had been damaged in the war, but was imposing nevertheless. Zora knew everything would be in Italian, but she didn't expect it to feel so Roman and Venetian.

It hit her that it was her family, really, who had been the newcomers here, even if it was over four hundred years ago. If the Italians really were about to give this up, it wouldn't be easy. Their roots went deep into the history of this disputed land. It was an unexpected perspective, and one she didn't dare share with her mother, who hated the Italians for forcing her to leave her home.

Medulin, a town of around a thousand people, was just a few kilometers away from Pula, and the bus took them east along the water. Soon, it stopped in a small center square between the sea and the church. There was a café with a table outside and a store selling vegetables on the corner. A few people got off the bus with them and quickly strode away in different directions. The building before them said La Posta and had a symbol indicating that it was the telecommunications center. The signs were all in Italian.

But still, it all looked strangely familiar to Zora. Her parents had talked about Medulin so much she felt as if she knew it, with its steep lanes rising from the sea, the tall church with two steeples on top of the hill, the stone houses gleaming in the sharp light. Here, there were no signs of Roman civilization, just a simple village, home to Marinovič and Rojnič for centuries.

Katarina and Zora hadn't brought much with them; it was summer and warm, and they planned to stay with family. At least her mother seemed confident that there would be room for them. Zora wasn't sure who would even be living there. After all, they had left over twenty years ago, when she was an infant. Since then, there had been the Italians, and the war.

Fig trees and grapes surrounded the homes above the square, and a dirt road snaked up to the church. Katarina strode boldly along the road, heading upwards. She wound her way along a few lanes and before Zora had time to figure out their exact direction, she turned left and they were on a path that led straight toward the top, where Zora could see a small square in front of the church. They slowed and then paused about halfway up, just as a slight man with thinning hair stepped out from a curved doorway on their left. Nothing about him seemed unusual, although he was dressed a bit better than she would have expected this far from the city.

"Bogdan!" Katarina suddenly shouted. The man reared in surprise and then his face shifted from oblivion through a slight tremor of fear to pure joy.

"Katarina! Katarina! Oh, my dear Katarina, I can't believe it's you! Roža . . ." he shouted through the gate, "Roža, it's Katarina. Hurry, come here!" He leaned momentarily back, looking for his family. Then the two of them — Katarina and Bogdan — stood, holding each other's shoulders, staring as if they needed to record every feature. Zora wondered what they saw in each other's eyes. When her mother started to tear up, she knew Katarina was seeing a lot more than just this aging man whom Zora would have passed in the street without notice. Bogdan, meanwhile, rocked back and forth from his heels to his toes in a trance like rhythm, his face in a large, disbelieving smile.

He finally spoke. "Where has the time gone, sister? And who is this one?" He stepped back and pointed.

"I'm Zora, Uncle Bogdan."

"Zora! Zorice! *Pa kako? Kako može biti?* But how? How is this possible? You are a lady! Do you know how old you were when I last saw you? You left here as a tiny bundle in your mother's arms. Let me look at you."

Now he put his hands on Zora's shoulders, straightened his arms, and started the strange distinctive rocking again. "*Pa šta si ljepa!* But how pretty you are!" His voice had a slight Croatian softening of the letter e, the *ai-kovka,* but there was also the trace of another accent. He didn't sound like their neighbors in Zagreb.

Almost immediately a young man some years older than Zora stepped out, and a woman about her mother's age followed, shrieking Katarina's name and grabbing her about the waist and dancing in circles. Both women had tears flowing down their cheeks. Without letting go of one another they stood, arms hugging shoulders, and stared at their children.

"So this is Zorića," said the woman, who was clearly Roža.

"And you are little Matte!" Katarina exclaimed.

The adults' tears kept flowing. It must have been a trait of all the women in their families. Zora could tell that Matte was as used to these tears as she was.

"Katarina, we didn't know you were coming. Why didn't you write? After all these years, we had given up on seeing you again, hadn't we Bogdan? What a blessing that you are here!" said Roža.

"We decided just two days ago," explained Katarina. "There wasn't time to write. Zora unexpectedly got some time off; she is taking a new job. So here we are. I had to see it all again."

"Yes, here you are. Where's Martin? How long are you staying? You'll stay with us, of course."

"We would love to stay with you," said Katarina, smiling at Zora. "And you know Martin, he still can't bear the thought of coming back."

Roža looked pointedly at the house across the street.

"Let's go inside," she said, "and hear all about you."

"I'll be right back," said Bogdan. "I just need to get something from the storeroom. Wait for me."

Inside, Roža put the Turkish coffee *jezva* on the burner, and they sat around the old olive wood table in the kitchen. The room was cluttered — an old sink, shelves full of dishes and pots, a large loaf of bread with jars of jam near it — but the late afternoon light flowed through the open door onto the old stone walls and gave it all a pleasant golden glow.

Katarina's eyes absorbed the kitchen she was raised in and she kept running her hands along the banged up side of the familiar table as if searching for a particular dent, or recreating a specific moment shared here. But Roža was clearly thinking of Martin's family home, across the way.

"It still hurts me every time I think about those people across the road," said Roža. "It is an awful situation. You know they won't give up the house, don't you?"

The relatives, to whom Katarina and Martin had "sold" the house across the street in desperation, had spent the time since the first war becoming more Italian than the Italians. And they had invented, as least as far as Roža and Bogdan could tell, a grievance against Martin and Katarina. They claimed to be owed even more land from Martin, for taking care of another relative, a deaf and mute brother. They had filed with the government to take over that land, but nothing happened, so they just shared their anger with everyone in the village. Their evil wishes extended to Bogdan, as well. They claimed that Bogdan had sold his house while he had been working in Croatia and illegally took it back on his return. There was no love lost between the households and Roža could barely look out her window without getting furious.

Roža told them she was sure these awful people had no intention of giving up Martin's family house and had ingratiated themselves with the local authorities to ensure that it was in their name. Now that the Italians were possibly leaving, they were nervous and had gotten newly aggressive on the subject.

"But we've never even thought about coming back for the house," said Katarina.

"I know. They are so unpleasant, we just ignore them. Let them stew a bit. I won't tell them why you are here; you can count on that."

"Why *are* you here?" asked Bogdan, interrupting his wife as he walked into the room, bringing a special bottle of *rakija* that he had made. He looked as if he had just realized there might be a hidden meaning to this trip.

"We're just here for a few days to visit with you," said Katarina quickly. "I want to swim in my sea, maybe eat some of our fish. And I want to hear all about your lives, find out how things are here. We've shared a few letters over the years, but there's nothing like hearing it in person."

Zora thought the answer came so quickly, it sounded almost rehearsed. Katarina had missed this home every day of her life, and now she talked about fish and swimming? Her mother had never before talked about swimming. For a moment Zora felt quite sure there was another reason behind this visit, but the fleeting thought passed, and she just stayed quiet. They all sat there, just looking at each other.

Katarina finally broke the silence. "Of course there is one other thing I must do." They all looked at her. "I need to visit the cemetery. I need to visit the boys, and my mother and father."

"You know we have been taking care of their graves," said Roža.

"Yes, thank you. It's been over twenty years since I have visited them. It's too long. My heart aches with the pain of missing them."

"I understand," said Bogdan. "How long do you have?"

"Just three days," replied Katarina. "Milena is getting married next week."

"*Bože moj*," said Bogdan. "Oh my God. Little Milena. Married. *Joj, joj*. Oh, my! Oh, my! Little

Milena. I've never even met her; she was born after you left. And now this!"

"And of course you already have grandchildren, Katarina." said Roža.

"Yes. I have five already. I think you know about my Rožića, my poor dear, the one we named after you. She died giving birth to her third child, bless her soul."

"I am so sorry," Roža reached out and put her hand on Katarina's. "There's nothing harder than losing your child. And you yourself have lost several, so you know better than I do. Is the little one, the one who was born as her mother died, doing well?"

"Oh, yes, they are all fine, thank goodness. You know Slavića went to take care of Rožića, stayed when the baby was born, and recently married Ivan. Maybe we should have seen it coming. She's pregnant with her own first child now."

"What? We didn't know all that."

"Really?" said Katarina.

"Slavića. Oh dear . . . Slavića . . ." Roža said, as if remembering something from long ago. "She was the one born right after you came back . . ."

Roža seemed about to say more, but Katarina interrupted, not letting her finish the thought. "Yes, our dear, dear Slavića." Katarina paused, lost in thought. "You know she was always Martin's favorite. And now she's there, raising her sister's children and about to have her own."

The interchange caught Zora by surprise. She had never heard about Slavića being her father's favorite. Zora always hoped it was she, herself, who was her father's favorite, but really, he loved them all. *What did her mother mean?* She wondered. And what had Roža started to say?

But the conversation had moved on, and Katarina was talking about Mara and Jana's children.

". . . So that makes five grandchildren for me, with a sixth on its way. You know, I am quite sure I wrote to you about it."

"I guess we haven't been all that good about writing." Bogdan looked at his wife, seeming somewhat sheepish as he spoke.

"It doesn't matter. We never were a family of writers. I'll tell you everything. But first you," replied Katarina. "What's happened here since the war? We try to read about it, but it feels confusing."

"Oh, it is confusing," said Roža. "But the good news is that we can speak Croatian again freely. It feels funny, after more than twenty years, I can tell you. We spoke it at home of course. But schooling was only in Italian. All business and all government was in Italian. It was dangerous to speak Croatian, and it got worse after this last war started."

"You know," Bogdan finally said, "I need to tell you something about your letters."

"What is that?"

"Well, perhaps the reason we didn't get them was that you sent them to Bogdan Rojnič. But that's not my legal name anymore. Those Italian postmen probably just threw away anything with a Slavic name."

"What?"

"Well for our family my name is still Bogdan, but I had to change it legally if we were to stay here. So I have an Italian name now. It didn't really help; I couldn't find work anyway. I wasn't willing to get that close to the Fascists. So I left and worked in the north of Croatia until the war." Now that he had started talking, it was as if the flow of words had waited for this moment. "But it's wonderful to be back home, and thank God we were able to keep our house in spite of everything. No thanks to your husband's relatives, mind you. We had some serious problems with that, as well, and almost lost it. They claimed I had sold it while I was gone." He finally paused to take a breath. "But I don't want to talk about the past anymore. Everything is going to be better now. I think the Italians will soon be gone."

He deeply believed this. And things were finally changing fast. Now that the days of the Italians were almost certainly ending, it didn't matter to Bogdan any more that his name had been changed or that someone had tried to take his house. It was over. For all of them, as for their country, the post-war period was going to bring a new world order, and they were ready to move on.

"You know, Kata, you might even be able to get your own home back."

But Kata didn't want to discuss it. She wasn't interested in old fights, and she knew nothing would change until the Italians were really gone. Her family was far away, and her home was with them now. They talked long into the night over many more coffees, lamented Martin's reluctance to come back while the government was still unsettled, and agreed to stay in closer touch in the future.

CHAPTER TWELVE
Medulin farewell

The call of a rooster the next morning pulled Zora out of a deep sleep. Her mother was lying next to her and as the room slowly grew brighter, the old stones in the thick walls and in the floor glowed. It felt comforting, and soon she heard her aunt pouring coffee and moving chairs in the kitchen. Zora went outside and brought in a pitcher of washing water. This was the room her mother had slept in as a girl, and Zora had felt her ease into the space as if she were putting on an old pair of slippers. Zora got dressed, then quietly slipped out and went for a short walk to give her mother and aunt some privacy.

By the time she returned, everyone had gathered in the kitchen over coffee. The sun streaming in the window lit up their faces, and warmth suffused the air and atmosphere. The old *jezva* that the coffee had been made in looked just like the one in the apartment in Zagreb, but everything else was different. The yard and the kitchen were like one extended room, and the flowers that Roža had put on the old table brought the garden scents with them. The furniture had been there long before any of them were born, and a lot of it looked like it was handmade from ancient olive trees or of pine from old forests that had now disappeared. Bogdan and Matte were at the back wall on a small bench, and the women sat on chairs with embroidered cushions. Katarina had her hand on her cushion, rubbing it in a way that told Zora immediately that her grandmother must have made all of them many years ago and that her mother had grown up sitting on them.

The old chipped coffee cups reminded Zora of her mother's kitchen, but Katarina fit in this place in a way she never had in the apartment in the bustling city center of Zagreb.

The conversation moved to things that were happening beyond this house. There were over twenty years for them to catch up on, and Zora was fascinated by everything she was hearing.

"You know," Roža said, "it's a very tense time here. Many of our people are still living in Croatia, just waiting to come home. The Italians who took over their homes and businesses are pretending nothing will change, but you can tell they are nervous. The ones who have family in Trieste are moving back there. Some of the small shops have already changed hands, and now they want people who speak our language at the counters again. We are, of course, very excited about the possibilities, but there's been so much turmoil we almost don't dare hope for too much."

"The political situation is definitely changing," said Katarina. "One reason Zora and I could come so quickly is that we no longer need a passport to visit here. Travel between Yugoslavia and Istria is completely open now, otherwise we would have had to wait for passports. I'm not even sure I know where Zora's birth papers are. Now that we are here, we can also go to the church and sort that out. I am not sure what Zora's papers say about her country of birth. Probably Italy. It was such a confusing time, when she was born."

"Oh, dear," sighed Bogdan. He had been just sitting and staring at her, but suddenly he was brought back to the present. "I guess there was no way you could have known. They are probably gone."

"What do you mean?" asked Katarina.

"The documents from the church are all gone. The Italians took them away. They wanted no record of the people who left. They didn't want you all to try and come back and reclaim your property. Everyone remaining had to file new documents at the town hall, in Pula. It was complicated and they tried to prevent us from doing it, and later said our house had been sold, just like they said yours had. But we persisted. That's why we finally have the papers for the house. It's also why I had to change all our names."

"Oh, my God," said Zora. "Does that mean I don't have proof of my birth?" She wasn't paying much attention when he talked about the house, but the remark about her documents being destroyed brought her focus back sharply.

"I'll look for that when we get back, *duše*," Katarina said. "You know, it was such a difficult time, your birth. We didn't know it then, but nothing would ever be the same afterward." Her mother looked at her with a distant expression, and Zora realized she was reliving a time Zora knew only from her mother's stories.

"That's right," Bogdan said. "Zora, you were born at the same time that Italy formally was given Istria and just before Mussolini became prime minister. We've waited the length of your whole life for that *prokleti vrag*, that cursed devil, to finally get his due. And now he's gone, and we are to be free of the Italian yoke at last."

"I am not even sure," Katarina confessed, "where the border is with Italy anymore. Are you?"

"Oh, it's moved pretty far away," asserted Bogdan, nodding his head. "You know even Trieste is no longer part of Italy. It's an independent protectorate of that new League of Nations. I think the Americans and the British are involved in overseeing it. Maybe we will get Trieste, too."

"I know. I was pleased to hear of that possibility," said Katarina. "There are so many of our people there."

"But the language in Trieste is mostly Italian, although there are many Slovenes there as well," said Bogdan, musing. "I passed there on my way back from Croatia. It still feels like part of Italy."

"They can have Trieste," declared Katarina. "As long as we get back Istria."

Her statement triggered a thought for Bogdan. "But what was it like living under the *vlasti* in Belgrade and the Serbs? Did you get to know them?" he asked. "It was very uncomfortable when I lived in Croatia. There was no love lost between many of the Croats and the government in Belgrade. It was especially rough just before the war, before I returned here, to get away from those *Ustaše*, those Nazis."

"Yes," Katarina said. "I'm afraid you're very right. But I hope we are moving past that . . ."

"Yes, Croatia broke away from Yugoslavia," Bogdan interrupted, needing to get it all out, "and declared itself a state, and joined with Hitler and Mussolini. A country at war with itself. It was awful. But that's over, those *Ustaše* have fled to Canada, to America, to foment their evil elsewhere. We will be one people, all Croats."

"You know, Bogdan, we have lived in both Serbia and Croatia since the Italians forced us out from our home here," said Katarina. "The Serbs took us in when we fled. They gave us a house in Petrovaradin; they gave Martin work. We would have been homeless and hungry if it hadn't been for them. They treated me like one of them. My daughters married Serbs. *Naši ljudi su; govore po našemu.* They are our people; they speak our way, in our language."

"You're right, Katarina. Besides, we aren't really even Croatian; we are Istrian. Our ancestors came from Montenegro, and we've been here almost four hundred years. I wish we could be our own country."

"That's not likely," young Matte spoke up for the first time. "We would be lucky to be a Republic or even an Autonomous Province of Yugoslavia. That's what we young people are working toward. But it looks more and more likely that we will be split between Croatia and Slovenia. Our part of Istria will most likely go to Croatia."

"Oh, Matte, you know Petrovaradin, where Slavića and her family live, is in Vojvodina, which is an Autonomous Province, just like Kosovo. I don't think you want that here. It's just one more reason to argue and fight. *Mnogi govore po Majarski,* many of them speak Hungarian. I'm afraid they will want to break away and go with Hungary. Martin and I are desperately tired of worrying about parts of countries breaking away and being at war with each other." Katarina paused, and looked at her brother, wondering what it had been like for them. She was so happy to be here, sitting in the same room with him, the wars over, the Italians perhaps leaving. Maybe peace would last longer this time; surely he and his son wouldn't want more turmoil?

"But we know we could be better off on our own . . ." Matte started to say when Katarina interrupted.

"*Basta!* Enough is enough!" Katarina raised her voice and seemed to grow in stature, more aggressive than Zora had ever seen her. Was this her mother, the peacemaker of the family?

Katarina continued, trying to contain herself. "Just keep your heads down until you are part of our country again. You are far away from the center, and you might be more vulnerable than it seems right now. You know Istria was taken away from us a few short years after the end of the First World

War, when we thought it was decided, and that we would stay in Yugoslavia. You don't want to risk that happening again."

"I know you might be right, Aunt Katarina," said Matte, wanting to ease the tension, "but we have to at least try and have our own identity." He stood up and started walking out of the house, barely pausing to hear Katarina's final comment.

"I understand," she said, "and you are young. But remember, anything is better than the Italians." She smiled then and almost ruefully repeated a phrase that no longer carried the old bite. "*Prokleti Italiani*! Damned Italians."

The next two days were filled, it seemed to Zora, with memories and Turkish coffee. The *jezva* came out, the coffee was ground, Roža made the same black thick liquid that Zora had grown up with. In this family it had never been replaced with the Italian espresso that was now served in public places. After dinner there was always *rakija*, the fruit brandy that no Balkan home was ever without. The first time Bogdan pulled out the bottle from the storeroom, he mentioned that he had always hated that *užasna grappa*, that awful grappa that the Italians favored. Clearly the years of living under the Italians had not endeared them to Bogdan and his family. Zora wondered how they would they feel once they were under Yugoslavia and the leadership in Serbia. Would they just transfer their resentment? Why couldn't their people live in peace, and just be happy in the embrace of their families? She wondered when it would all end, this conflict.

Every day Katarina walked up to the cemetery, while Zora went down to the sea and explored the town. Only the first time did Zora join her mother. The cemetery was small, and the graves had simple stones over them for the most part. Many were old and crumbling, and the ancient trees above them dropped branches and leaves.

Katarina cleaned up and put flowers on the graves of her parents and of Martin's parents. It was only when they stood over the smaller stones that Zora realized how little she knew of the boys: just the two names: Vjekoslav, meaning *glorious through the ages*, and Dragutin, *the dear one*. She knew they had died during the First World War, but no one ever talked about them; perhaps it just hurt too much. Even this time, Katarina said little.

"Mama, how did the boys die?" Zora finally asked near the end of the visit while Katarina just stood and prayed, silently.

"They died of influenza," Katarina said simply, with almost no emotion. "Or so they told me . . ."

"We were in those terrible camps, just before the end of the war. It was such an awful time, so much pain, so much evil . . ." She turned away even as she answered. Zora suspected her mother was crying, but Katarina would never let her daughter see that deep sorrow.

The way she spoke let Zora know they would not be talking about her mother's time in exile, about what had happened when she and the children had been deported during the First World War. Katarina was different in the cemetery, withdrawn, almost a stranger. She retreated to a place that didn't include anyone else, and it was clear she wanted to be alone. This, from a woman who normally surrounded herself with children, who reveled in their company, who, by choice, was almost never alone. Who told stories, and who wanted Zora to know about the past. Clearly, this was not a past that she was willing to share. It was a Katarina that Zora hardly recognized.

So Zora explored the town on her own during her mother's visits in the cemetery. She walked to the water and took her shoes off, waded in. She wished she had thought to bring a bathing suit. There were fishermen about, and a few children running and swimming. But it was pretty quiet. It was pleasant enough, but she couldn't imagine living there. She would quickly miss the vibrance of her city, the cafés, and the young men.

On their last night in Istria, when Zora and Katarina were alone in the room where they shared a bed, Katarina talked about the importance of having all her daughters speak her language. Zora wondered if that was easier to talk about than all the rest of it: the pain she felt about her boys; having to leave her homeland; and part of the family in Vojvodina, still at some risk of being taken over by the Hungarians. It seemed odd, how tied both her parents were to language. She had never felt much concern about the issue; Serbo-Croatian was just the language spoken everywhere she had ever lived, and she didn't give it all that much thought.

"*Biti će mi lakše*, I will rest easier, when Yugoslavia regains all the lands that were taken away after the first war and during the second war. I won't have to worry about my grandchildren having to speak some foreigner's language," Katarina said.

"What about religion, Mama? Is that as important to you as language?"

"The Communists have taken religion away, and there are many who are upset about that. But you know, Zora, it's not important to me," confessed Katarina. "Our ancestors were part of the Orthodox church in Montenegro, and in Istria, at some point long before my birth, we became Catholic. Now our religion is supposed to be Communism. I don't really think any of it matters. We know in our souls how to be good people. That is all that is important, in the end. It will be less about who won which war and more about how much love we shared. I want you to remember that, Zora. Teach your children that all war is evil. Only love matters."

"You are right, Mama," agreed Zora. She had really never heard her mother be so reflective, and wasn't sure how to respond.

"But promise me, *duše*, that you'll work as hard as I did to make sure your children speak our language so we will always be linked together. It's the one thing that has tied us to our people for all these hundreds of years."

"Of course, Mama. Why wouldn't my children speak our language? Now that the war is over, we're all one country again. Besides, I have to get married before I think about what language my children speak," said Zora, dozing off.

CHAPTER THIRTEEN

Losing Katarina

Zora felt her mother's energy flag on the way home to Zagreb. She assumed it was just the exhaustion of the trip, and the deeply emotional time she had spent in her hometown, with her family, and the memory of all her loved ones in the cemetery. It would be better, she thought, when they were all together again.

Upon their return, Katarina updated Martin on all the changes. He was sorry to hear about the feud with his relatives, and that it had spread to include Bogdan and Roža. How tragic that they were fighting over houses and land, when he had given up everything and made a new start. He now realized he could never go back, even if the Italians left. It was a bitter taste, the residue of that eviction and displacement. Now, it would just be too painful to return.

Katarina's energy, meanwhile, didn't revive, and a visit to the doctor confirmed the worst — the cancer had spread throughout her body.

She told Zora first, since they had just spent those special days together. Zora suspected, then, that Katarina had known what would happen, and that it had pushed her to make that last trip home. Suddenly many things about the trip made more sense. She was grateful to have shared that special time with her mother and that she saw the land that had been so dear to both her parents, the place where she herself had been born.

A few months later Katarina died at home, surrounded by the family she had protected and sacrificed so much for.

To the last Katarina never complained. She just kept telling them how happy they had all made her. She said over and over again, "*Vi ste moja sreča I radost.* You are my joy and good fortune."

Katarina never saw Istria returned to Yugoslavia, but she saw enough when she visited to believe that it would happen in the near future. That was good enough for her; it reassured her in her final weeks. Katarina also knew, deep inside, that her husband needed to stay with his girls now that she was leaving them.

Istria was the land of her birth, but Yugoslavia as a whole was the homeland of her daughters. Martin was safe and at home.

PART II

Zora

CHAPTER FOURTEEN

A best friend's wedding

For a year after her mother's death, Zora missed her all the time. She was the oldest one living at home. Ljuba was continuing her studies. Milena and her husband Dule lived nearby, in his mother's apartment. Martin had retired, but he just didn't have the same spirit after Katarina died. He stayed healthy and spent his time in the café with his friends. He no longer cared much what he ate even though Zora tried hard to cook his favorite foods the way her mother had.

Zora loved her work at the telephone exchange. She was soon the lead person on the Zagreb-to-Belgrade link and felt personally responsible for keeping that voice traffic flowing. Yugoslavia was growing stronger, and it was important for Zagreb, the capital of Croatia, to stay linked to the capital of the Republic in Serbia.

Zora was grateful that they had lived in Petrovaradin, in a Serbian speaking area, all those years of her childhood, because her knowledge of the Cyrillic alphabet gave her an edge up on the telegram communications that alerted them to issues that might arise. The language of the Republic was Serbo-Croatian, and both the Croatian, or Latin-based alphabet, and the Serbian, Cyrillic alphabet, were broadly used. But there was no doubt that the Serbs were in charge, and they insisted on Cyrillic. They wanted to maintain a strong relationship with Russia, or rather the Soviet Union, and having the same alphabet and a Slavic language helped.

Zora also knew that the management in Belgrade was very comfortable talking to her and considered her very competent. Her bosses didn't spend time wondering whose side her family had supported in the war, or whether Zora's relatives still resented the fact that the capital of the country was in Serbia. Zora sounded like one of them, and they assumed that she was reliable.

She really hadn't given the issue of language, or what flavor of Serbo-Croatian she spoke, all that much thought in the past. But now, as she saw how she was benefiting from sounding Serbian, every once in a while she had the vague idea of asking her father about it. She just wasn't sure why her family had let her grow up speaking Serbian when they spoke Croatian. She guessed that as long as it was a Slavic variant, they wouldn't care. Or maybe they liked that link to their past in Montenegro. In any case, she had started school in Serbia, and she sounded like her schoolmates by the time they had moved away. With Croatia joining the Nazis during World War II, it was a minor form of protest for her to not change her spoken expression to sound like them.

Her parents, she knew, had always been obsessed with speaking "their" language, rather than Italian or Hungarian, but she and her sisters avoided the subject as much as possible. They spoke Hungarian because they had lived near that country, in Vojvodina, with many Hungarian neighbors. They didn't hate Italians or the Italian language like their parents did. And it wasn't a subject they wanted to argue about. They didn't miss Istria because they had never lived there. They didn't want to live in a backwater next to Italy. They were young and liked being in the heart of the city of Zagreb, which was really recovering quickly from the war. Everyone around them had always spoken Serbo-Croatian, so it didn't feel like a threatened language to them.

There was even a saying Zora had learned while going to school in Serbia: *"Govori po Srpski da te ceo svet razume."* It meant "Speak Serbian so the whole world understands you." She didn't know where it came from, and it could even be that her teacher meant it seriously, but she and her friends always thought it was funny. They had studied enough geography and history to know how little Serbia was and how few people in the world understood their language. But they also knew how proud Serbian people were. So Zora would use this one phrase ironically, as a way to bring things back to reality when her friends let themselves get too arrogant about something.

But life for Zora was about so much more than language and politics. Right now her best friend Draga was getting married and had invited Zora to be her *kuma*. The *kuma* and *kum* were the bridesmaid and best man, but it was also a commitment to be godparents to the children from the marriage.

Draga was marrying Josip, a young man from Belgrade. They had been seeing each other since before the war, when Draga's family had also lived in Serbia. Draga's father moved the family back to Croatia when things got dicey between the two countries, worried that his Croatian roots would make it harder to keep a job in Serbia.

Draga and Josip had maintained their relation-ship, aided by the fact that she could talk to him on the long distance connections. Josip worked at a small electrical equipment company in Belgrade that was owned by some White Russians — as refugees from the Communist revolution of 1917 were called — who had lived there all their lives. Zora had met Josip when he visited and enjoyed the time they all spent together. But she had some concerns.

"Oh, Draga." Zora said while trying on the outfit she would wear for the wedding. They were at the home of a neighboring woman who had sewn Draga's own beautiful pale pink wool suit. Zora had wanted to sew her own, but Draga convinced her that this would be more special. Of course she knew Zora would pick beige, so she had selected the rich plum fabric herself. "I am so excited about you and Josip, but you're mov-ing so far away. And aren't you worried that he works for those Russians?"

"Oh, Zora, *mila*, dear, I will miss you when I move. But since we work for the phone company, you and I will be able to talk to each other, and you can come visit us. And no, I'm not worried about the Russians. Josip has told me all about them. They are good people; they're just like us."

The seamstress had left the room to alter a seam, and Zora continued. "I don't know. My father is concerned about the Soviet Union, about how their influence is spreading."

"I understand. But these people aren't like that, you know," said Draga. She and Josip had talked a lot about the people he worked with. Draga had met them, and thought they were interesting—and handsome. She couldn't wait to introduce them to her best friend. "Their families fled the Communists years ago. They all grew up here and would never go back. You know Josip has asked Tolya, the younger brother, to be his *kum*. They grew up near each other and were in technical school together. He's very special. You'll see—you'll get to meet him when he comes for the wedding."

The seamstress came back in; the altered suit fit perfectly, and Draga was thrilled she had picked the warm-toned fabric. Zora looked beautiful in it.

CHAPTER FIFTEEN

Meeting Tolya

Draga and Josip's wedding in 1946 was small and intimate. The timing, at the end of summer, was perfect, for Zagreb was at its best. It was warm, and the days were long.

The traditional and elaborate ceremony was performed in the Orthodox Cathedral, unknown to Zora before that time. The priest wore a long gold robe and had a beard; deacons swung incense holders, and a choir sang in the back of the church. Draga had converted to the Orthodox religion of Josip's family. None of the young people felt strongly about religion, and Draga easily agreed to the conversion since Josip's grandparents were religious.

At the celebratory dinner after the wedding everyone toasted: "*Živeli!* Cheers!" and sipped *rakija* until they could barely stand, and then they all danced the traditional *Kolo* circle dances.

Draga and Josip had other dinners with the family and a few close friends. Of course Zora and Tolya, the younger partner in the electrical firm, were included in all the events. Since Draga and Josip wanted time to themselves as well, Zora and Tolya inevitably ended up spending a lot of time together. In addition to eating and dancing, they talked.

Zora learned that Tolya had trained as an engineer, and that, like Josip's, his education was interrupted by the war. They had both served briefly in the Yugoslav cavalry, but as the Germans defeated Yugoslavia in a matter of days, they didn't see much action.

Zora had never even met a Russian before. She quickly concluded, however, that he didn't seem foreign to her at all. Besides, he was tall, dark-haired and handsome. And he had a gentle smile and beautiful brown eyes—eyes that couldn't stop looking at her.

At twenty-nine, Tolya was five years older than she was, and had grown up in Serbia because his family fled the Bolshevik revolution when he was an infant. He and Zora had a lot in common. Both had been forced to flee their country of birth because their people lost a war. Both grew up never knowing the place their parents had lived in for centuries but still held dear. Both loved the country they had grown up in, considered themselves natives, and had no desire to ever leave. Both had jobs they liked, which were challenging and had good potential.

Tolya's family, like Zora's, had moved several times within Yugoslavia as his father looked for work. Now, with his father dead and his brothers married, Tolya lived with his mother in the heart of Belgrade, not far from Zora's sister, Jana.

Zora and Tolya also both had families obsessed with "their" language. Tolya's father had died before the Second World War, but his mother insisted on maintaining the language, religion and tradition of her Russian Cossack ancestors. Tolya spoke Russian fluently. He had gone to a Russian boarding school that the Yugoslav government set up for the immigrants under the assumption that they would eventually return to Russia when the Communists were defeated.

Instead, the Communists had not only retained control over Russia, they had taken over Yugoslavia. The émigré Russian community was devastated. They hated Communists almost as much, if not more, than everyone had hated the Germans.

Tolya had no more interest in going back home to Russia to live than Zora did in making her home in Istria. As far as he was concerned, Yugoslavia was his country, and he was building a good life there.

There was a lot of structural reconstruction after the war ended, and for a time Tolya had worked around Tuzla, in Bosnia, laying electrical wires. He always spoke fondly about life in Tuzla and of his friends there — the *Musulmani* — as the Russians called Moslems. Eventually he had moved back to Belgrade to work with his brothers, and their electrical workshop in Belgrade was thriving and growing.

Since Tolya had come all the way from Belgrade for the wedding, he stayed almost a week, exploring Zagreb. By the time the wedding festivities were over, Zora and Tolya were interested in getting to know each other much better. Zora brought Tolya home to meet her father and Ljuba.

Martin remained skeptical about getting close to a Russian, but Ljuba couldn't stop talking about him. "Oh, my God," she said, over dinner a few days after he left. "He's so tall and handsome! Zora, why do you always get the tall, handsome ones? Or are you going to tell me 'he's just a friend?'"

"I'm not sure, Ljuba," said Zora. "This one could be something more. But he lives in Serbia. I haven't been back there since we moved here almost ten years ago."

"What will you do?"

"Well, for a start, we're going to talk on the phone a lot," she said with a fond smile on her face.

"They have a line in their workshop, and of course I have access to the country's long distance network!"

"I imagine you are already making your coworkers blush with your conversations," said Ljuba.

It was Zora who blushed as she looked at her father. "Well, not exactly."

"But *duše*, he's Russian," complained Martin. "I really liked that Croatian young man you were seeing last year."

"Oh, that wasn't serious, *Tata*! Besides, does it really matter where his family comes from?"

"Well, you don't speak Russian, for one thing."

"But he speaks Serbian, *Tata*. I have no trouble communicating with him."

"Didn't you say he speaks Russian with his family?" asked her father.

"He does speak Russian with his mother. But *Tata*, he's Josip's *kum*; they are best friends. He's part of our community."

"And isn't he Orthodox?"

"Yes, but I'm not sure he's any more religious than I am . . . or than you, for that matter."

"He lives far away. That's a lot of things he's got going against him," Martin insisted. "Are you sure he's worth the effort?"

"Oh, he's certainly worth the effort, Tata. We can talk for hours, and I never get bored. I really like him. Please try and stay open-minded," Zora pleaded.

A month later, in October, Zora was heading to Belgrade for a brief visit. She told her father it was mostly to see Jana's new son as well as to visit with Draga and Josip, but everyone knew Zora would be spending a lot of time with Tolya.

The trip settled everything.

There was no question in Zora's mind about her future. Tolya was the one for her. She had introduced him to Jana, met his family, seen his apartment, and, ever practical, visited the Belgrade headquarters of the telephone exchange. She was a swirl of emotions, but her most important task now was to talk to her father.

"How was the visit, honey?" Martin asked. For a rare moment, it was just the two of them in the apartment.

"Oh, *Tata*! Tolya's asked me to marry him!" So much for planning the discussion carefully.

"Marry him? But, *duše*, you've only known him a couple of months, and you've spent less than a week in his city! He can't be serious."

"But he is, *Tata*. And so am I. I said, "Yes!""

She got out the *jezva* without which there could be no conversation with her father. Heating the water and grinding the coffee gave them something to do while Martin absorbed the news.

"You want to marry a foreigner from another city? A man you barely know?" Martin frowned. "A few weeks ago you were worried about Josip working for those Russians, and now you want to marry one?"

"Oh, *Tata*. I know this man." Zora sat across the table from her father, and reached for his hand. He just had to understand how she felt. "I've been with other men, and I know the difference. Tolya is the only one for me."

"So you've made up your mind?" Martin should have expected it, but it felt so sudden. He suddenly missed Katarina more than he had in months. What would she counsel him to do? "Don't you want to talk about it?"

"I'd love to talk about it, *Tata*. I can hardly think about anything else. But I have made up my mind. If you want to talk me out of it, then let's not."

"What would your mother say?" Martin felt lost. This wasn't easy, and he didn't know the answer to his own question.

"I don't know, *Tata*. I hope she would be happy for me." Zora too, wished her mother were there. But it was because she wanted her to know things were going to be all right. "You know she wanted me to marry and have children. He wants lots of children, just like I do."

"But she meant for you to marry one of our men, to speak our language with your children."

"*Tata*, I'm not even sure who 'our' men are. Do you think she would have liked me to marry a Croatian nationalist, an *Ustaša*? Or a Serbian partisan who's now in the Communist party? Don't you think she would just want a good man for me? And we've talked about language. He knows I will always speak *po našemu*, in our language, to the children," Zora insisted. "I promised Mama that."

Suddenly Martin knew his wife would have supported Zora in her choice. She always supported him and the girls in whatever path they chose. That's why he had loved her so much.

"I did really like Tolya, " he said, smiling and putting his arm around his daughter. "I just worry that you are going into this so quickly. Will you wait a while before getting married?"

"Not really, *Tata*." Zora smiled at him. She knew this was hard, but she saw no reason to wait once she had made up her mind. "I went to the telecommunications headquarters in Belgrade while I was there. You know I have worked closely with a number of the people in that office. They've offered me a job. It's a good position, I'll be even more involved in this new technology that is changing the world. I'll make more money, and I can start next month."

"Next month?" Martin's coffee cup clattered as he put it back on the saucer. "But that's so soon!"

"I start on November first." Zora spoke quietly and just looked at her father. "I can live with Jana until we get married."

"And when will that be?"

"On November twenty-second." Martin was silent. Zora stood up and walked next to her father, bending down and looking in his eyes. "Please give me your blessing and be happy for me."

"Oh, *zlato*, golden one," Martin wrapped his arms around Zora and finally gave her the only blessing she needed. "I am so happy for you. It's wonderful to see you excited."

"But what about his family?" Now he started wondering what it would be like for her to leave him and their home for an unknown family. "Are they pleased? This is rather sudden for them, as well. At least I met him a couple of months ago. They've just met you for the first time. And while I know you are wonderful, I also know how protective mothers can be of their sons."

"Well, to be honest, his mother didn't seem all that thrilled." Zora didn't want to go into the details with her father; he was concerned enough. "But Tolya's quite determined, even though he is very gentle most of the time. He told her he had made up his mind, that he wanted her support, but that he was going ahead with it with or without her blessing."

"Oh, *zlata*, I'm so sorry. What about his brothers and sister?"

"Well, his brothers are married to Russian women, but his sister married a Serb. So at least he's not the first to jump a boundary. I liked them all; we really got on well."

"I suppose," said Martin, "that it's normal for them to marry our people. After all, they've lived their entire lives here."

"His sister is pregnant with her first child; it's due in a few weeks. So the first grandchild will be half Serbian."

"And my next one," he smiled, "could be half Russian."

"That's right, *Tata*," Zora said. "And I did promise his mother I would change my faith to Orthodox and raise the children that way."

"Oh, well, that's not too important." Martin didn't really have to think much about this. Religion just wasn't a big issue in their household. He couldn't remember the last time he had been to any church. "Our families were Orthodox in Montenegro, and your sisters also converted when they married Serbs. You won't be the first."

"I also promised," continued Zora, "to learn Russian. Really, it will be a self-defense measure. It's all they speak at home. I don't think it will be difficult. I already picked up a lot of words." She was actually excited about this. Zora had always loved languages and learned them quickly.

"So you're happy about this?"

"Oh, yes, *Tata*!" Zora beamed. "And I meant to tell you, he loves to fish and will take you with him whenever you come visit us!"

"Well, if he loves to fish, he must be a good man!" Martin declared. "If you are certain, then I am with you all the way. I think I hear Ljuba walking up. I need to go rest a bit while you tell her. By the way, she has some news for you, too."

"Really?" Zora rushed to the door.

Ljuba thought it was all very romantic, of course, but her mind was on other things. She had just been offered the opportunity to spend a year in England, going to university. All her expenses would be paid.

So the family had a lot to celebrate that night. They invited Zora's sisters, Milena and Mara, and their families, and stayed up until way too late, talking and celebrating everyone's good fortune. For there was another momentous event. That evening,

Milena told them she was pregnant. It was the first time since they lost their mother that everyone was happy, and Martin was feeling good, surrounded by his girls—women now. He'd think about the fact that they were all leaving him later.

Zora and Tolya's wedding picture, Belgrade, November 1947

CHAPTER SIXTEEN

Belgrade and marriage

Zora had understated her concerns about her future mother-in-law. Tolya tried to prepare her, but no preparation would have been enough for Daria Pavlovna Romanov.

"She's a *Cossachka*, you know," he said, as they had stopped in a café while walking from the train station in Belgrade to his apartment. Tolya used the Russian word for a female Cossack, as if this would be explanation enough. "They're tough, these Cossacks, and in my experience their women are even tougher. But don't worry, it will be all right."

"What do you mean, 'they'? Aren't you a Cossack as well?" Zora had learned a lot about the Don Cossacks over the last few months, for it was as much a part of Tolya's cultural identity as being Russian.

His family had lived for generations on the Don River, in the south of Russia. It was a land of rolling plains and wide rivers. The small villages made up of simple *isbas*, or hay-roofed huts, were widely dispersed, and the men rode horses long distances. The people were loyal to the Tsar and would risk anything to protect that culture.

The Cossacks were a fiercely independent community, and the first and final group to fight the Communists as part of the White Army. Tolya's immediate family had long moved away from the nomadic past of their ancestors and were small landholders and grain merchants who barely escaped as they lost the war in 1920, when he was a child of two. They had fled to the Black Sea—with five children and a grandmother. At the last minute, they ended up in the town of Evpatoria, where the Don Cossack Host, as the military arm was called, were being evacuated. It was November of 1920, and the White Army was finally acknowledging defeat. Because Tolya's father Ivan had served in the war, they were taken to the Greek island of Lemnos by a military minesweeper—the T-412, which was captured by the British and given to the White forces. At the end, his grandmother had refused to disembark and returned to Russia, never to be heard from again.

As far as they knew, they were the only family to escape their village when the Red Army, as the Communist forces were called, defeated them. They waited almost a year in an overcrowded tent camp on Lemnos for any country that would give them refuge. Finally, the King of Serbia decided to take them in, for there had been close ties between the Slav countries and their royal families. Yugoslavia was to take in over a hundred thousand Russians, and set up schools and organizations for them.

The Cossacks all became part of a global Russian diaspora, with an émigré organization that had elaborate plans for the defeat of the Communists and a return to Russia. They ran military academies for the boys and boarding schools for the girls. It was a way of life that preserved their Russian culture, frozen into a pre-revolutionary fervor.

"Well, you know, *zolotko*," said Tolya, using the Russian endearment that meant golden one, "all this militaristic behavior is not for me. I want to live in peace. And I don't want to be in the middle of these infernal Russian *dela*, or affairs. I'll tell you more about it later, but it's not a group I want to be enmeshed in. I've been in this country since I was a baby, and I left all that behind when I left the Russian *Cadetsky Corpus*, or military boarding school. They raised us to believe we were all just waiting here to go back home, but I'm not going back to some god-forsaken village in the heart of Russia. I like living here, in a large city. This is my country."

"I'm glad," said Zora, laughing, "to hear you aren't planning on going back to Russia!"

Zora met the whole family when she went to visit the flat Tolya shared with his mother. It was where they would live when they married. Apartments were still very hard to come by in Yugoslavia, and they were fortunate there were two bedrooms. Right now, Daria Pavlovna had the larger room, but Tolya had assured Zora they would move into it, rather than the monastic room he had shared with his brother Kolya until his brother's recent marriage.

Daria Pavlovna's was not a warm welcome. The tall, black-haired, strongly-built woman glared at Zora whenever she thought her son wasn't looking. Her long hair was tightly braided and wrapped around the back of her head, not one hair out of place. She wore a long black dress and sensible shoes. Small gold stars dangling from pierced ears and a gold cross around her neck were her only jewelry other than a plain gold wedding band. She looked down on Zora from her superior height as if their size difference established superiority and reflected the appropriate relationship between them.

Zora knew she was most likely reading too much into this. The woman was tall and therefore had to face downwards to talk to Zora. She did seem relieved that Zora at least spoke Serbian and not Croatian. The Serbs and Russians had always been tightly linked and shared a religion and an alphabet. The fact that Zora had agreed to convert to the Russian Orthodox faith from her own Catholicism didn't impress her; in her mind it was the only option.

The formidable oldest brother, Shura, was even taller than Tolya, himself over six feet. He was clearly the man in charge of the family fortunes. His wife Galya, a laboratory scientist at the hospital, was working late and couldn't come. Shura was a bit aloof in bearing, but clearly loved his younger brother and wanted to support him. If he approved of her, Zora thought, their mother would have to go along.

The next brother, Kolya, was the antithesis of these two handsome men of military bearing. He slouched, had a slight paunch already, and greeted Zora with a gentle smile. His wife, Lyolya, on the other hand, was a tall, beautiful, patrician Russian who might have been a princess in their previous world. She smiled sympathetically, as if she could easily imagine what Zora was going through. Kolya also worked in the family *radionica* or workshop, but he didn't get involved in technical problems. He basically talked to the customers and kept the place orderly, if Zora understood correctly.

Sister Liza—physically a younger version of her mother—and her husband Mika walked over from their home just down the street. Almost nine months pregnant, Liza was anxious to get back home. However, Zora felt great sympathy from her, as well.

Daria Pavlovna, who was of such icy formality that she had required the use of her full name and patronymic even by her husband, was dressed in mourning black although that gentle man had died some years before. She knew Serbian but preferred to speak Russian and have her sons translate for her. A torrent of Russian words would flow from Daria Pavlovna, as if bursting from behind a dam of frustration. Tolya would synthesize—or recast—it all to just a short phrase or two, usually innocuous enough. He would then change the focus and bring Zora into conversation with the young people, easing the tension. Zora determined then and there that she would learn Russian. She had agreed with Tolya that their children should speak both languages, so she needed to be fluent.

Tolya had also told her that his mother was an appallingly bad cook who insisted on eating only Russian food. She was already worrying that her future daughter-in-law didn't know how to make *borscht*, beet soup, *pirozhki*, fried meat buns, or even *seledka*, the pickled herring that made vodka go down more smoothly.

Zora couldn't believe that she was not only marrying, but adopting a martinet of a mother-in-law. It certainly made her realize how fortunate she was in her own mother. Mama had been such a warm and sweet woman, and all her daughters and sons-in-law adored her. How did Tolya turn out to be such a wonderful man with that woman in his life? It did probably help explain why he had that strong backbone under his gentle humor and kindness. Actually, that was what made him irresistible to Zora. The fact that he was almost glamorously handsome didn't hurt either. She had fun thinking about the wonderful children they would have, mixing her steely determination and his more flexible approach.

She did have a few moments of doubt that weekend, and wondered if she would have been so ready to accept the whole proposition had she met Daria Pavlovna first. But Belgrade really wasn't that far from Zagreb, and she would continue working for the phone company, which could lead to trips back to see her family. And Tolya really didn't seem in the least bit foreign. With her sisters and her friend Draga nearby, and Tolya's siblings so friendly, life in Belgrade would be an adventure without being a radical break from the life she had built over the years.

Or so she imagined.

Sasha with Zora and Deda Marinovič.

CHAPTER SEVENTEEN

The golden child

Nine months after the wedding Zora and Tolya's son Sasha was born. Sasha, short for Alexander, was named for his Uncle Shura, yet another nickname for Alexander. Zora and Tolya were beside themselves with joy. Tolya's first nephew had been born the day of their wedding, and Zora already had two young nephews in the capital, so they were surrounded by family and babies. Fortunately, Sasha was a quiet and easy baby from his first days. And of course he was brilliant.

While Zora, now living in Serbia, was busy recovering and learning how to take care of a newborn, her father and other Istrians were celebrating a vital moment in the life of their own country.

On September 15, 1947, just four days after Sasha's birth, Istria was formally reintegrated into Yugoslavia as part of Croatia and Slovenia. The northern part went to Slovenia, and the largest piece, including Medulin, went to Croatia. The Istrians celebrated in spite of the fact that many young people, like Zora's cousin Matte, had wished for a separate state of their own. At last, they were free of the horrible yoke and persecution that started when Mussolini came to power just after Zora's birth in 1922.

Not everyone rejoiced. Many Italians now lived in Istria. Some had been moved into Istria after the first war and had displaced Slavs like Zora's family, but others had been there for generations. Now a reverse persecution started, and many were moving back to Italy, in a forced reverse migration. It seemed there could be no shift in that geopolitical landscape without pain to some part of the population.

Zora's father regained some of the land he had owned—the pieces closer to the sea that had no houses on them—but the Marinovič family home stayed with the relatives who had moved in when the family fled. They were not about to give it up and even resented the parcels Martin regained. It hurt Martin to think about them and this feuding. He knew he wasn't going back to live there, but he had hoped that ridding themselves of the Italians would bring a deeper sense of connection to his homeland. Instead, there was this permanent reminder of how things had gone wrong.

The acreage Martin again owned had some fig trees and grapes on the most buildable plots. The land was flat and had rich soil and gorgeous views of the water. Sometimes they vaguely talked of building a summer home there, where everyone could gather and celebrate the family and their heritage.

Meanwhile, Zora was happily living in Belgrade. Daria Pavlovna had grudgingly moved into the smaller room. Zora was used to large families and tight spaces, so just four of them in the apartment felt like a luxury. She hadn't brought much with her from Zagreb—a few embroidered and crocheted pieces her mother had made—but the apartment looked familiar. It was simply decorated, with worn furniture and old pots and pans. She did buy some new cake pans when she realized there were no implements for baking her *torte,* cakes.

Daria Pavlovna never lifted a finger in the kitchen, and Tolya was ecstatic to discover that Zora was a fabulous cook. She quickly developed an expertise in Russian cooking, trading recipes with her sisters-in-law. Tolya also loved the food she had learned from her own mother, especially her *sarme,* stuffed cabbage, and the delicious *torte* she made in the new pans.

Zora learned to speak Russian fluently and with no accent, and easily fit in with the rest of Tolya's family. Sasha grew quickly and was a model baby. His dark hair, eyes and complexion were definitely Balkan in character according to Zora's family, and seemed quite Cossack-like to the other half. He smiled easily and — most reassuringly — almost never cried. He walked early, and not only talked early, but spoke two languages before he was a year old. He spoke Russian with his father's side, and Serbo-Croatian with Zora's family and their friends. Zora just assumed this was what having children was like. The only other infant she had helped raise, her youngest sister Ljuba, had also been bright and easy.

On Sundays Sasha and his father would stroll to the café together, Tolya bending sideways so his son could reach up and hold his hand. Sometimes people would look at Tolya on the street quizzically. He would laugh and have Sasha introduce himself to them. It made him very proud. In the café, each would sit with a section of the newspaper, as if they were both reading. Tolya would pour a beer and Sasha would get some foam in a small glass, just like his father.

Daria Pavlovna fell in love with Sasha and became his caregiver while his parents both worked. Zora was doing well at her job and was also thriving as a wife and mother. Tolya's business was growing, and they were getting involved with the new electrical appliances that were starting to appear in the country. Sometimes Zora would go visit Jana and her new baby—a second son—and they would laugh and talk about how sweet life was.

Last picture of Sasha and Tania before the family fled Belgrade. With cousin Mima on right.

CHAPTER EIGHTEEN
Cold War threatens

For a time after Zora and Tolya's marriage, the political situation in Yugoslavia eased. The leader, known as Marshall Tito, enjoyed a degree of global esteem and was slowly leading the country to a more liberal version of Communism than his friend Stalin was in the Soviet Union. It seemed like maybe everyone could relax for a while and rebuild their lives.

But about a year after Sasha's birth, in the middle of 1948, relationships between Tito and Stalin started to change, and not for the better. Stalin was leading his country on a disastrous path, creating fear and devastation instead of letting them slowly recover from a war that had killed millions. His secret police were notorious, and people were spying on each other. A series of labor camps, or gulags, were set up

173

in the same parts of Siberia where the tzars had once imprisoned opponents.

The tzarist banishments paled in comparison to the stories that started coming out of the Soviet Union. Millions of people were being deported without warning or trial. The secret police — the Checka and then KGB — were everywhere; neighbors spied and reported on neighbors; children were taught to report on their parents. One or two letters had come from near Tolya's home village, followed by silence. His grandmother was never heard from, and there was no way to search for her.

Stalin was furious with Tito's bid for more independence and neutrality. In 1948, Czechoslovakia threatened revolt and was brutally brought into line. But Yugoslavia was beyond his immediate control. He would have to invade to get the blind obedience he insisted on. And invading would be harder now that the aftermath of World War II was winding down and America was getting protective. Nevertheless, tensions rose.

None of this should have been an issue for Tolya and his brothers. They had emigrated to Serbia as infants to flee Soviet Communism. They hated the Soviet Union and all it stood for.

But things were never what they should have been in the Balkans, and the situation was especially sensitive in those days of early Cold War jockeying. Shortly after the schism between Yugoslavia and the Soviet Union, White Russian émigrés in Yugoslavia started being accused of spying for the Soviets. Some were rounded up and evicted from the country, others put on trains back to the Soviet Union. If that happened, they would be either summarily shot as traitors or sent to the gulags, the infamous work camps in Siberia.

Soon after, all White Russian refugees, regardless of how loyal they were or how long they had lived in the country—or even whether they were married to Yugoslav women—had their citizenship revoked. They were granted a one-year permit to stay in the country, theoretically renewable, but no one knew anything for certain.

Then the situation grew worse. People who spoke Russian were carefully watched, sometimes by neighbors. Several close friends of Shura's were deported. Anyone with a Russian name was suddenly at risk. Zora was pregnant with her second child, and fear and worry endangered her health and the baby's. She and Tolya spent hours talking about what they could do.

Since Zora was from Istria, in Croatia, they considered going there for a time, seeing if things might settle down further from the capital. But moving about between the states required paperwork and permission, and right now they had to keep their heads down and hope things might resolve themselves. In addition, they deeply believed that if they had to leave their home, they would do all they could to ensure a future for their children that was free of this constant turmoil they had both endured their entire lives, from earliest childhood. Chaos was the only consistency in their lives, and they wanted something better for their children.

Shortly after that, however, the pressure became insupportable. A Communist party man who was a major client of the business told Shura and Galya that he would be happy to "buy" their apartment and "manage" their business for them. They got the message. They could "sell" to him and leave, or they would be forced out, and it might not be to a place of their choosing.

CHAPTER NINETEEN

Tania born to crisis

As her pregnancy neared its term, Zora feared that their situation could only end with escape. The claustrophobic aura tightening around them — in what had so recently seemed like a world of new beginnings — was crowding out the joy she desperately wanted to feel, but couldn't, about this new life forming inside her.

Zora's ongoing pregnancy didn't help in managing the risks of their situation. Intense conversations between Tolya, Shura, Kolya, and their mother seemed endless. Their sister, Liza, having married a Serb, felt more secure — her sons were Serbs, and had a Serbian last name.

One night, Zora heard their loud voices through the wall of her bedroom. Their apartment was often the gathering place, since with her pregnancy, Tolya took extra care to stay at home as much as possible.

The walls between the rooms weren't thin, but the sitting room was right next to their bedroom, and tensions were high enough that their voices carried.

They were up late, and she was almost due. The four-kilo mound that would soon be her new baby struggled to get comfortable in her womb, just as she struggled to get comfortable in the bed she normally shared with the man who was arguing with his mother and brothers in the kitchen.

She had heard it before, this debate, but its intensity was increasing. "I am a loyal citizen," Zora heard her husband shout, "I fought in our army, why would they arrest me? I have nothing to do with Stalin, I curse the ground he walks on. We fled them thirty years ago; we would be killed if we return to Russia."

"Hush, Tolya. *Oni*, they, are probably listening," whispered Shura.

"If 'they' listened they would know I am not a risk to them." Tolya was defiant.

"You have to tell Zora there's no alternative," even Kolya was determined they would all go together.

"She knows; she knows." Tolya sighed. "I just hope she doesn't decide she and the children won't come with us. She could just go back to her father and leave me to my uncertainty."

Of course Zora knew. They had talked about it endlessly. Tolya was angry, but it was for fear of putting her and the children at risk as much as potentially losing everything he had spent a lifetime building.

The pains then wiped everything else from Zora's mind. Tolya ran into the room, and got her quickly to the hospital, which was luckily nearby. The next thing she really remembered was a baby girl emerging, screaming as if some need to protest had infused her every molecule.

The new child, conceived in hope and born into fear, should have been loved and cosseted. She might have, had she been delivered to a happy couple making a new life, like her brother had been, less than two years earlier. But those calm days were gone and nothing was to be the same again. And she was as different a baby from the calm boy who preceded her — her older brother Sasha — as it was possible to imagine.

Fat cheeked and chubby, everything about her was noisy. She gurgled when happy, and screamed when she wasn't. Squirming was her style, and she fell out of her grandmother's arms often enough that the old woman quickly tired of trying to comfort her. The requisite dark eyes were mysteriously linked with pale — nearly white — blond hair so fine that it felt like the down that flew from the comforters when Zora shook them out. Who could she possibly have taken after?

I was that new child. They called me Tatiana: *Tatjana Anatoljevna*—or in Cyrillic—Татьяна Анатольевна. A mouthful of a name in either language or alphabet, but an easy Tania for short. My first name had the advantage of being Russian, but my mother's favorite name as well. The advantages, it seemed, ended right there.

I was born in the middle of 1949, into a family in turmoil. My mother's older sister, Jana, had a daughter, Vesna, around that time. Vesna and I were born in hospitals in the heart of Belgrade, and came home to apartments nearby.

Vesna came home to a certainty about life that I was not to know for many years. A calm and quiet baby, she was the third child born to a family that combined Serbian and Croatian parents, but was fully Yugoslavian. She was welcomed into a country that grew stronger on the world political chessboard, but one that didn't have room for my half-Russian family. For our first years, at least, it seemed that of the two of us babies, she had won the lottery in life.

I was a very difficult child who cried endlessly and loudly, and developed slowly. For most of my life, when she was particularly frustrated, Zora would remind me that, had I been the first, there might not have been a second child. She forgot to mention that the family's circumstances around the time of my birth were uncertain to an extreme and not conducive to bonding. For six months the family's entire future was in question. Would we leave or stay? Would we make it safely? Where could we go?

And how long would it be before anyone felt safe again?

TRIESTE IS A HAVEN FOR NEW WAVE OF REFUGEES

From G. E. R. Gedye — Exclusive to "The Mercury" in Tasmania

TRIESTE.—A new and pressing problem has arisen for the Free Territory of Trieste out of the fact that Marshal Tito is busily putting his house in order. The difficulty is how to cope with the new wave of refugees, who are reaching this little occupied zone at the rate of some 500 a month.

* * *

LITTLE more than a year ago, the displaced person population of the zone was only 200; the big influx of fugitives from Yugoslavia had long died down and between 1947 and 1950 the thin trickle of fugitives —mostly anti-Tito Yugoslavs—was easily dealt with.

But in January, 1950, the tide began to rise again, so that today Trieste's four D.P. camps have a population of between 4,000 and 5,000. This strains accommodation and other resources to the utmost.

The new arrivals, among whom I have been spending a day here, are not so much refugees as deportees. The great majority of them are Russian "Whites," refugees from the Bolshevist Revolution of 1917; many of them ex-members of the Denikin and Wrangel armies, who have been living for over 30 years in Yugoslavia.

The starting point of their new troubles was the inclusion in Moscow Radio's daily torrent of invective against Marshal Tito of charges that he was maltreating these anti-Soviet Russian "Whites." Moscow's indignation at Tito's alleged harshness to Moscow's oldest enemies was boundless.

Belgrade Radio promptly announced that if Soviet Russia would dry her tears long enough to send a dozen empty trains to Belgrade, the Yugoslav authorities would gladly ship the whole lot of Tsarist Russians back to their land of birth.

* * *

THIS offer was ignored. But Marshal Tito declined to risk this hypocritical pretext being used to stir up more feelings against him. Just over a year ago he started clearing the Yugoslav decks for action in case of invasion. Since then, the tempo of deportation has increased month by month.

Although nearly half the refugees are Russian "Whites," the opportunity has obviously been taken to get rid of other "undependable" elements.

Usually the deportees are given three or four weeks to settle their affairs before boarding either an eastwards or a westwards train, as they please. A few to whom I spoke had been plundered. But I saw one hut in the Opcina D.P. camp here packed from floor to roof with refugee baggage. Many have brought out furniture — one even a grand piano! Others arrived destitute.

The Russian (and many other) refugees are mostly of the "white collar" class. There are, for example 60 doctors among the present inmates. Some are talented musicians; the orchestra in one of the smartest night bars in Trieste consists of Opcina D.P.s.

The administrators of the Trieste D.P. camps are achieving wonders with their limited means. One thing that, of course, they cannot do is to make them anything but D.P. camps, the precarious refuge of the derelicts of this age.

* * *

THE great ambition of every inhabitant is to find a new fatherland as distant as possible from those they have lost — and from Trieste.

CHAPTER TWENTY

Exiled again

But of course there was no alternative. Exile. Again.

My father's brothers and their wives left Yugoslavia in the late summer of 1949, a few weeks after my birth. My parents, along with my brother Sasha and my father's mother, Daria Pavlovna, waited a few months, until I was old enough to travel.

We spent some time with my grandfather Martin—*Deda* Marinovič—and Mama's sisters in Zagreb. Mama would be leaving behind her sisters, her father, and a lifetime spent in the belief that her family had endured their final forced flight. Half of the sisters, including Zora, were in Serbia, while the others were in Croatia, in Zagreb. But all of them were safe in a united Yugoslavia, and it was only Zora's husband's Russian ethnicity that now threatened her immediate family and forced this flight. She was leaving her country to join a diaspora composed of Russians fleeing a revolution that ended thirty years earlier but whose consequences affecting her family just would not end. It wasn't her battle, but Tolya was her husband and therefore her future lay through the path of this crisis.

Martin was haunted by memories of Zora's own birth. The parallels were strong, both families being forced into exile, both mothers with new infants. But he was worried that the future for Zora was even more uncertain now. At least he had known where he was going, and that the new country, Yugoslavia, had offered shelter. There was no such certainty now.

"Are you sure you want to do this, *draga*?" Deda asked Mama when they had a moment alone.

"*Tata*, I really don't have any choice." They had tried everything they could think of to stay in the country. Mama's boss at work had petitioned to get her family special classification because she was a vital worker, but it did no good. "Tolya and the children can't get their Yugoslav citizenship back, and if we stay he could be deported to the Soviet Union. And you know how insane Stalin is. We have to leave," said Zora.

"Yes, we've been reading about it." He sighed. "You know that if you go, there's no coming back."

"I do, *Tata*. We have actually already crossed that divide. The children and I gave up our citizenship to get permission to leave. It was the only thing we could do." Zora spoke in short sentences with long pauses in between. It was the only way she could keep the tears at bay.

"What does that mean?"

"It means we are stateless. We have no papers."

"Nothing?" The finality of the situation was sinking in for Martin. He might never see his daughter and her family again. Just like he had never again seen his own birthplace.

"Nothing. We are lost souls. I almost feel like a character in a Russian novel," she continued, trying for a bit of humor to ease the discussion. "No identification papers, no passport." Zora told him she was able to sneak a copy of our birth certificates, translated into English, into the lining of a coat. She also had made a copy of all our identification cards translated into English before my father was forced to turn them in.

"Why English? I thought you were going to Trieste?"

"We are going to Trieste. There's a camp there, a Displaced Persons camp, sponsored by the United

Nations, but mostly funded by the Americans. We can live there until some country agrees to allow us in, and we are doing all we can to ensure that country is America."

"That is so far away, *duša*. Why America?" asked Martin.

"It's the only place in the world where our family will be safe from the long reach of Stalin, *Tata*. We want our children to grow up in peace. I want them to know about their heritage, but I want them free of the constant tensions and threats that accompanied our lives here."

"But will America take you? And how long will it be before you know?"

"They have a quota for those who have been made stateless by persecution, *Tata*. We hope it's just a few months. It shouldn't be very long." They had all already filed papers to get visas to the United States. "And you know, there are already many Russians in America who will sponsor us and help Tolya get work. Engineering is a valuable skill everywhere, and it's a tight community. We'll be all right, *Tata*. In a few months I will be writing you from America about our new lives." She wasn't sure how realistic all this was, but she didn't want her father worrying. She was as committed as Tolya to create a new future for her children. They had to get away from this turmoil that kept invading her Balkan homeland.

"Oh *draga*, America is so far away!"

"I know, *Tata*. But after everything that's gone on here for our entire lives, we want to get as far away as we can. I wish I could stay here with all of you, but it just isn't possible."

They had been sitting on the bed he slept in, which also served as the sitting area in the daytime. Now they moved to the kitchen, and Zora got the *jezva* and started the coffee.

"You know, I once dreamed of going to America," Martin sighed. He hadn't planned on talking about this.

"You did? I didn't know that."

"I never told anyone. It was when Mussolini was kicking all the Slavs out of Istria. I thought, *Why not go far away, away from all this madness*? But your mother wanted to stay in a country where they spoke our language."

"You know, when I promised her my children would speak her language I never envisioned this happening. But I'm determined that they still will," said Zora.

"But *draga*, they will have to speak English if you go to America."

"Of course, but they can speak my language as well. I'm their mother, after all."

"And will Tolya want them to speak Russian?"

"Is the sun rising tomorrow?" Zora laughed. "Of course. That family can't imagine a world where Russian isn't their language. If they didn't give it up in thirty years here, they won't give it up now, especially since they are being forced out *because* they are Russian." She was happy that her father had moved on to talking about language rather than what might really await them at the end of the train ride to Trieste.

"So which language will the children speak?" Martin continued.

"Why both, of course. Sasha already speaks Russian as well as *po našemu.*"

"He does seem like an exceptionally gifted child."

"He is. I am so lucky!"

"But Zora, you are talking about three languages, not two. They will speak our language, Russian and English? And you will be the only person in their lives who speaks our language. Are you sure about this?"

"When we're in America," Zora continued, a phrase she would use for far longer than she could imagine at that moment. "When we are in America, everyone will speak English. It will be easy for them to learn. And besides, they are so young. Tolya and I have talked about it a lot. We think it will work."

"Well, you are fortunate with Sasha, but what about the new one? The one that's been keeping us up all night?"

"I don't know, Tata." Zora smiled ruefully and shook her head. "That one is angry. She hasn't given me a minute's peace since she was born. I hope the Americans will take her!" She was only half joking.

"Well, you can hardly blame her, Zora. It's not as if she entered a world that was peaceful and calm."

"True. I just hope she'll grow out of it," Zora said, almost wistfully. "Things will be easier when we're in America, I'm sure."

"Oh dear, I hope they take all of you and quickly," Martin said. "How will you get to America? Have you been able to take any money with you?"

"We have a little, and Tolya is hoping he can work in the camp while we are waiting. Tolya is bringing his camera and developing equipment. He was quite passionate about photography before all this started, and he bought a wonderful camera, it's called a Leica. People will need pictures for their documentation and visa requests. There's also an organization that helps Russian refugees."

"Oh?"

"Yes, it's called the Tolstoy Foundation. It was set up by Leo Tolstoy's daughter after the author's death, and they help pay for people's relocation if they have been left homeless after fleeing the Soviet Union."

"Thank God for Tolstoy, then," said Martin. "We would love to help you, but you know we have nothing. Things are still very tight here in Zagreb since the war; we barely have enough to survive."

"Oh, I know, *Tata*. We aren't looking for anything from you. We have to do this on our own. We will. Don't worry." She kissed him and they hugged. Then I started crying again and the moment was interrupted.

But *Deda* wanted to know one more thing. "How are you getting along with your mother-in-law? Are things better?"

"We've more or less made our peace, *Tata*. She's not like a mother to me, but she loves Sasha and is good to him. It helps a lot that she can take care of him, and he loves her. He can't say the word for grandmother—Babushka—so she has become Babusya. I'm just grateful not to have to call her Daria Pavlovna anymore. We all call her Babusya. Another gift from my lovely son."

"Well, I am glad to hear that. It could be tight quarters for a while."

"Oh yes, we understand we will be sharing very tight spaces in Trieste at the camps," explained Zora. "And she makes no secret of how much Tania's crying annoys her."

And so, with me crying, in two days we left the country of Yugoslavia, and all my parents knew and loved, for perhaps the final time.

Sasha and Tania shortly after they moved to San Sabba

CHAPTER TWENTY-ONE
Campo San Sabba

"Ti si uvek plakala. You were always crying," the story started, as did so many others that Mama told about me as a baby. They weren't about the hardships, or the fear, or even about Sasha, her golden child. They were always about my crying.

The train to Trieste crossed the border at night. The border was lax, because the Yugoslavs were happy to be rid of the Russians, and Trieste was accepting refugees. At the time, Trieste was a so-called Free Territory under the United Nations and governed by international law, administered by British and American forces. The refugee camps there had been set up in the aftermath of World War II, to deal with people displaced and unable to move back to their homes, primarily East Europeans and Russians.

Zora remembered that when the train arrived in Trieste, people without passports were crowded into one part of the station. From there we were taken in the back of a truck to the processing center for Displaced People. It was about half an hour out-of-town, up a hill, in a place called Opicina.

The truck pulled in past a raised metal bar into a field full of old dark green tents surrounded by woods. One wooden barracks at the front had a sign that said *Ufficio*. Inside, at a desk, were people who spoke Italian and a little Russian and Serbian. It took forever to fill out all the paperwork, but they were very happy that Zora and Tolya had hidden copies of our old documents, even if Yugoslavia had declared us all non-citizens.

Finally, the new documents were finished. Our family was now officially registered as stateless. We possessed new refugee travel documents, issued by the United Nations Committee on Refugees based on something called a Nansen Passport. It would be used to identify us until we were accepted on a permanent basis by some country. Everyone assumed it would be a matter of a few months. Tolya, in fleeing Russia as an infant, had already been issued one of the original Nansen Passports, but he no longer had it.

Everyone was then taken to the tents where we would stay until we could be processed into the longer term DP, or Displaced Person camp down in

Trieste. That camp was at an old rice granary called San Sabba, near the shipyards. The Opicina camp was normally to be used by families with young children in the summer, when it got swelteringly hot in San Sabba. But there were so many unexpected refugees still flowing in that we had to be put up there first, with several thousand others.

We were given blankets and pointed to an area in a large tent that we would share with other families arriving at the same time. There were no beds, as there had been no warning of another arrival. Newcomers simply laid out their blankets on the ground. We did that and fell asleep as well as we could.

Too young to remember that arrival in early 1950 in Campo San Sabba, I heard Mama talk about it so often during my childhood that I could visualize it just by closing my eyes.

I was never a hero in Mama's stories. She believed that if you complimented your children, they would get swelled heads, so she never did. But I loved her tales of the old country anyway, even if I came off less than the stellar child that was her firstborn.

"There were so many things about those first days I can never forget," Mama continued, "but I specifically remember trying to settle the five of us into that small space and mostly I remember you crying."

I was less than a year old. We had been on the move for a good part of my life, and now we were to be crowded in a drafty barracks until some country took us in. "We are going to America," Mama's story went on. "I kept saying it to anyone who asked. I believed that if I said it often enough it would be true."

That first night was to be one of many in the Campo — way, way, too many. A truck took us from the tents at Opicina to Campo San Sabba, where my Russian aunts and uncles were living. But they were in the large brick building across the street from where our family was headed. They lived in the old San Sabba rice factory, long decommissioned and now packed with refugees. We couldn't live there because no children were allowed. So we were on our own, heading for the barracks in the camp annex. My parents knew there would be other Russians from Belgrade in our camp, but they had no idea who they were.

Mama knew for certain, however, that she was the only non-Russian person among the "displaced."

The part of the camp where we were headed was a large flat field filled with long narrow wooden army barracks abandoned by the American military after the end of World War II. A tall chain-link fence surrounded it, the wires extending into the distance as far as could be seen. As we pulled up, the gate was opened by a gentle-looking man in his fifties. He had no uniform, but wore a military looking cap. We climbed out of the back of the truck. Papa carried the few suitcases — everything we owned. Mama carried me. Sasha walked next to us. Babusya carried her own suitcase and followed.

"I remember there was a sign in Italian that said *Campo*, and *Profughi*, and other Italian words I didn't understand or have time to read. But I knew this was where we would now be living." Mama's stories always brought me right back to the Campo, and sometimes I believed I remembered it all, from the very first day, even though I was six months old at the time.

On arriving in front of the Campo, Mama just stood before the gate and stared. It was late evening, and two big lights glowered over the scene. The ground between the barracks was barren dirt. These temporary shelters were spaced about ten or twenty steps apart from each other, in long straight rows going off behind the barracks that served as the Campo headquarters office. A few larger buildings lined the field across from the headquarters. Someone told us they included the medical center, the school, and the kitchens where meals could be picked up. Everything looked a bit shabby in the stark light.

A small group of people stood around, watching as our group of new arrivals listened to the introductory comments in Russian and Italian. And then the driver of the truck read names. As each name was read, one of the people watching responded with a smile. About forty people lived in each barracks, and they were there to welcome us newcomers and introduce us to the rest of the people who lived in our barracks. Mama didn't know, at the time, that this was something the refugees had come up with, a way to make newcomers feel wanted. It was a godsend. After months of insecurity and not knowing what the next moment might bring, suddenly someone was welcoming us, someone who was living through a similar situation.

A young couple smiled as Zora and Tolya's names were called. "We are the Karsanidis and this is our son Sasha," the man said, pushing a small boy forward.

"I'm Sasha too!" said my brother. The boys looked at each other shyly, then Sasha Karsanidi walked over to his new friend — my brother Sasha — and gave him a marble. It was clear glass with green and blue swirls. Mama said she worried briefly about how small it was, and whether Sasha, at two and a half, might swallow it. And then she saw him beaming proudly as he held it out to show it, and she felt something that had been held tight loosen in her. At that moment she started the slow process of understanding that this group of people was now her family.

Zora had left her father, her sisters, and her friends in Yugoslavia along with all her possessions. There was no going back. Our only documents now were the Nansen Passports that declared us stateless. But here we weren't the only ones officially homeless. Everyone in camp had faced this same situation, most of them, like us, more than once.

The Karsanidis led us to our barracks, not far from where we stood. A few people were gathered before the door. They introduced themselves, welcomed us in. We walked through the door at the center of the barracks to a small open area, which held the bathrooms. A narrow corridor led off in either direction, and we turned left. Plywood walls that reached neither the ceiling nor the floor— broken up by doors every few feet—lined it. We passed a few doors and reached the last one on the left. Like the one across from it, it swung freely when pushed. In the doorway on our right, across the hall from our home-to-be, stood a large woman

in a dress that was too tight, too short and too
bright.

"I'm Vava," she said, in a voice that was rough, as
if from smoke and shouting in noisy places. She
smelled of cigarettes, and it was one of the few times
Zora was ever to see Vava without one in her hand.

"I'm Zora," Mama said. "And this is Tania." She
pointed to me, the baby in her arms. I had quieted
during our walk and was now asleep, and she
whisked me into our new home. Babusya followed,
holding Sasha's hand. Papa brought up the rear with
our bags.

Zora thought the apartments in Yugoslavia had
been small, but at Campo San Sabba she walked into
a space no bigger than eight feet long and six or sev-
en feet wide. Behind it was a second space the same
size, with two sets of bunk beds lining the walls. The
first room had a small stove, a table, and a ban-
quette. At night Babusya would sleep on the ban-
quette. In the daytime it would be our family room.
The remaining four of us would sleep two to a cot
under old khaki military blankets on the small lower
bunks in the rear. The upper bunks would serve as
our storage area, holding our clothes and anything
else we possessed, which fortunately wasn't much.

It was late and everyone was tired. Mama got us
into bed as quickly as possible, unpacking only

enough to get us through the night. Sasha and I settled in on our side of the room. "You started crying, Tania," remembered Mama, "and you cried, and you cried, and you cried."

Mama brought me into their bed, but I didn't stop. She walked me up and down the narrow space between the bunks, but I didn't stop.

The partial walls were so thin she could hear the neighbors tossing and turning. She was mortified at what they must be thinking. Tolya and Sasha slept through it all. They always did. Mama was up most of the night, with no private space to retreat to. I would quiet down when she gave me her breast, but I'd start up again as soon as I was done. This went on endlessly. Zora couldn't find a way to stop whatever it was that bothered me. She never could.

Near dawn Mama finally closed her eyes as I crawled out to the other half of our small space. I found Babusya's bag to play with and was quiet. Zora could hear people getting up. The neighbors, not too quietly, were talking about the crying baby, angry that it had kept them up all night. Zora drifted into slumber at last.

When she woke up, she realized that it was still morning and there was still no crying. Sasha and Tolya were asleep. She put on her robe and stepped out to check on me. Babusya was there, but I was not in the room.

"Where is she?" Mama asked.

"Isn't she with you?" Babusya replied.

Mama ran to the door and shoved hard. It slammed into the wall behind it, startling everyone in the entire barracks, for sure. She was oblivious. Suddenly she heard a familiar—but too rarely heard—little giggle. It came from under the door across the hall. Zora knocked on the door.

"Yes?" The door swung open. It was the man who had let us in at the front gate the night before, the one with no uniform but a military cap. There was nothing loud or threatening about him. He had greying blond hair and gentle blue eyes.

He was the kind of person you could imagine telling fairy tales and singing lullabies. He stepped back and to the side so Zora could see the whole room. Behind him, on the floor, sat Mama's giggling baby daughter—me—playing with the old gent's cap. Two elderly women sat on bunk beds in night-dresses and hairnets, enchantment on their faces, staring at the scene. The termagant in the tight dress stood at the other end of the room, putting on bold red lipstick.

"She is such a sweetheart," one of the old women, whose name we later learned was Tama, said.

"What were you doing to her to make her cry all night? She's such a happy baby!"

This happy baby apparently cried her way through the first year of her life. I cried when we were at home. I cried when we weren't at home, and when we no longer had a home. I cried when we were on trains. I cried when we weren't on trains. I cried.

Until, that is, I met *Dyadya Zhenya*, Uncle Zhenya, the man with the cap. Apparently, I thought the sun rose and set with him, and the feeling was mutual and immediate. We were inseparable from that moment on.

Clearly, all believed that my crying was Mama's fault, and they now had indisputable proof that this was true. The minute she tried to take me across to our end of the barracks, I started bawling again. It would not be the last time my mother was to be blamed for my behavior.

Sasha and Tania with her beloved Dyadya Zhenya when he was
on duty at the guard station at the entrance to the camp.

CHAPTER TWENTY-TWO

Campo family

"*Prestani*, Tania. I wish you would stop crying," Mama nearly shouted, exasperated. It was many months after that first night in the Campo. "You're old enough to tell me what you want. If you need something, just ask."

I was barely two, and she knew she was being ridiculous. She also knew they were all laughing at her behind her back. Damn it, she just wanted her daughter to start talking.

"Of course she's not talking, Zora," said Vava, picking me up and hugging me close until I quieted. She was always one of my champions. "She can't figure out what language she should use."

"Oh, how absurd!"

"It's not absurd. What do you think, Zhenya?" Vava asked her uncle and barracks-mate. "Her father and everyone else around her speaks Russian, and you, but only you, her mother, speak to her in Serbian. I would be confused, and I would be angry. Why can't you just talk to her in Russian like everyone else does? Then maybe she'd be talking instead of crying."

God damned Vava, thought Zora, *she always thinks she knows everything*. She had never held on to a husband, never had a child, but here she was, telling Zora how to raise her kids. And poor Zhenya. She had him wrapped around her finger like a kite on a string.

"You know, I don't have time for this conversation right now," Zora said. "I need to go wash clothes and get some food ready. Sasha is coming home from school soon; he'll be hungry."

"Sasha, Sasha. Your little genius. He's got you wrapped around his little finger," sneered Vava. "Go ahead, you can leave Tania with us. We'll take care of her. Won't we, Zhenya?"

Zora couldn't believe she threw out that phrase. She was a gypsy, that one, Mama knew she was. She read the future in coffee grounds, but she seemed to read the present just by looking in Mama's eyes. And Mama never was good at dissembling.

Zhenya just smiled gently, as he always did.

That morning they were all sitting as they usually did, having Turkish coffee in the pergola outside the door to the barracks where twenty families were crowded into rooms with all the privacy of public toilets in a train station. The doors didn't shut tight, there were no locks, the walls might as well have been made of paper. There was nowhere to think, nowhere to breathe. These people knew every detail of Zora's intimate life, every detail of how she was raising us. For all she knew, they could all read her innermost thoughts. And right now those thoughts were not very gracious.

She knew she left me to them too often. She knew they believed she favored Sasha, my older brother. *But damn it*, Zora thought, yet again, *why does Tania have to be so difficult?*

The thought no sooner entered her conscious mind than she rejected it out of hand. Of course she loved me. But life was so hard there, what with not knowing where we were going or when. It had started before I was even born, this unsettled existence. Zora knew it wasn't my fault, and she knew it would get better some day. She just had to get through it somehow, the best she could.

"Thank you, Vava. I really appreciate it that I can leave Tania with you. I hope she doesn't pester you too much." Zora's mind settled as she said the words, and by the time she finished, she knew she meant them.

She was lucky to have these people sharing the space across the hall. Thank God they loved her children. Four childless adults all past middle age, vaguely related to each other, permanent refugees from the endless wars of a cursed century, they could have made her life much more miserable. Instead, they were tireless caregivers for her challenging daughter, who far preferred their company to her own Mama's.

Everyone knew I never cried with them.

They don't have to take her to the clinic to get her shots, Zora thought. But she knew this was ungracious, a way to try to justify her somewhat fractious relationship with me, and apologized again for having to leave me with them so often.

"Oh, she's never a pest!" Zhenya said. A lifelong bachelor, a Russian émigré like everyone else at the camp, he made me the light of his life. Mama knew I would be fine with them. She knew I'd start talking when I was ready, and I would speak her language and everyone else's. Sasha had spoken both languages before he was a year old; he didn't find it confusing. But he grew up surrounded by both languages. Now, Zora was the only one speaking Serbian in a world of Russians.

Zora had promised her mother, Katarina, on her death bed that she would raise her children speaking their language. It had seemed easy, then. She knew how important it was to her mother. Katarina felt they had given up everything back in Medulin, to protect themselves from the Italians who were trying to kill the Slavic language and culture. To her, it was like trying to kill her soul. She never learned another language, and couldn't imagine what that would be like. Thinking and talking and breathing all happened in Croatian, for her. It was her mother tongue.

For four hundred years she and her ancestors had protected the language while all else changed around them. It was the one known, the one tie that they would not sever. Zora had promised that her own children would know the security of that solitary constant and she intended to live with that promise, no matter what environment she had landed in through no fault of her own.

Zora headed to the central kitchen to get lunch ready. When she returned with the food for our meal, Vava greeted her joyously.

"*Progovorila*! She spoke!" Vava cried. "In Russian, like we knew she would."

"*Šta je rekla?* What did she say?" Mama asked, in Serbian, of course. These Russians had all lived in Serbia for thirty years after the Russian revolution, and they all spoke the language fluently, if reluctantly.

"Well," Zhenya explained, "Tolya walked by on his way to his darkroom and when he greeted Tania, she said, '*Papa!*'"

Of course, thought Zora. *It had to be.* All children say *Mama* first, but not her daughter. And not, *Tata*, or father in her language, but *Papa*, in Russian.

Enough! She forced her mind forward. *Be happy she is talking.*

She walked into the barracks, then down the hall to our quarters. Everyone looked at her, and then at me. "*Papa!*" I said, pointing at my father.

"*Kako lepo*, How nice, Tania," Mama said to me, in Serbian, hugging me close. No baby talk in the camp, interestingly.

"*Tata je došao kući? Tata came home?*" Zora asked me, *po našemu*.

"*Tata kući!*" I affirmed, *po našemu*.

That brought the house down. Two sentences, two languages. I was my Mama's girl!

"Tolya, Tolya," Zora shouted, as if he wasn't right there next to her. "*Progovorila ye, istina, progovorila ye!* She's talking! It's true; she's talking!"

And from that moment on, I spoke. Easily. Constantly. In two languages. I used Russian with my father, my grandmother, my uncles and aunts, in the pre-school, and with everyone in the camp. And, miracle of miracles, I spoke Serbian with my Mama.

No one else, just Mama. It was our language. Our private link.

I could change languages in mid-sentence if I stopped talking to Mama and started addressing anyone else. It was as if I'd been storing it all up, skipping that silly baby talk stage of just having a few words. When I was ready to start, I started — when I had something to say.

Mama wanted to believe it was special, having our own language, a language no one else used. And it was, in its own way. But really, she knew I was still much closer to Zhenya and Vava and the two aunts than I was to her. I would slip under our front door and into their space whenever I wanted.

She had to confess, she told me often later in life, that with my blond curls and round face, my giggly laugh and my impious humor, I brought joy into all their lives, lives that needed joy. Even if she had the ability to hold me back, she couldn't imagine doing so. Both our barracks and our camp was a happier place because I was, in effect, the camp mascot. I would spend afternoons sitting with Zhenya at the entry gate, for his job was to let people in and out of the camp. I would put on that silly cap of his, walk up to the gate, and give a sharp salute when a stranger walked up. I was the only one there who didn't know we were living in a refugee camp or that our lives used to include adequate food and apartments and bathrooms and kitchens that weren't shared. I had never known another life. It was my world, and I thrived in it.

Sasha did fine, as well, but he was just living a normal life. I was reveling in mine.

Well, most of it, anyway. I thought the camp food was pretty boring. Every day Mama went to the kitchen and brought back cafeteria food. In the morning there were powdered scrambled eggs, from old American military kits left over from World War II, and we kids had cocoa. For dinner it was spaghetti one day, the next it was rice, the third it was polenta. There was a bit of tomato paste, some bread, sometimes meat. Mama tried to get vegetables in town whenever she could.

I loved spaghetti, and Zhenya did as well. On spaghetti days everyone gave Zhenya anything extra and on the days in between he would heat it up and the two of us would eat it at his dining table. I never got tired of eating pasta with him every day. The camp food wasn't very healthy and my first set of teeth, which lasted until I was almost ten, were actually brown stubs. While later in life I would have many opportunities to regret the lack of minerals in my diet, as a child I never complained as long as I had my spaghetti.

But the thing that killed Mama the most was how much I loved Vava. Why I seemed to prefer this creature to her was confounding.

Picture a really loud, overweight woman in her early forties with big hair, big features, big red lips. Now imagine a cigarette hanging out of the side of her mouth. Picture a dress too tight at the hips and too low in the bosom. Add a hard, raucous laugh. Now imagine this as the pre-school teacher, taking your daughter away every morning. Your daughter holds her hand as she happily skips down the front steps, the two of them chattering away like old best friends.

Vava was Zhenya's niece, and he, too, adored her. Tama was her mother, and Sonja was her aunt. Vava had left a husband somewhere in her past, and her father had left Yugoslavia to fight the communists with a group of Russians who joined a German brigade in World War II. He was never heard from again.

This odd foursome — Vava, Tama, Zhenya and Sonja — was my second family, and they became Mama's, too. You choose your friends, but not your family. It was true of the family Mama was born in-

to, and it was true of the family that adopted us in
these odd and difficult circumstances.

Sasha outside the hospital in Trieste that Zora and Tolya had to
sneak him out of because the Italians were being paid by the day
while he was in the hospital

CHAPTER TWENTY-THREE
Sasha in Italian Hospital

"Tolya!" Zora called one morning while waking Sasha for kindergarten. "Sasha's stomach hurts and he has a high fever. We need to take him to the clinic!"

Tolya was startled, because Mama was usually very reluctant to take us to the clinic. I would howl at the very word, for to me it was associated with the big needles that stabbed my butt and left me unable to sit for days. Zora always took our illnesses in stride, and mostly cured them with hot chamomile, so Tolya knew this was serious.

Two days later Sasha was in the nearest hospital, outside of Campo, in the city of Trieste. He had an appendectomy, and while recovering was diagnosed with the flu and put in a quarantine unit. Then things got really frightening. Not only did Zora and Tolya need permission to leave the camp, once they got to the hospital, they weren't allowed to visit him.

And of course there was no way to call the hospital, so they just kept making the trip and getting turned away. One day they saw him through the window of his ward. He was lying on a small cot in the middle of a long room with a handful of other little children. A nurse walked around, talking to them. The sight of her son through the window, now a skinny little boy in a gray cotton shift that looked like prison garb or worse, had Zora nearly in tears. She knew he could see her, but could do no more than smile and wave.

Finally Mama and Papa arrived at the hospital one day and were told they could visit Sasha. Many of the other beds were now empty, and it felt lonely and cold. They ran into the room, Sasha jumped up from the bed, they all hugged and then Zora did cry. Sasha was still skinny, but he looked so much better. Zora was sure he was well and needed to come home. It had been a couple of months, but felt like years.

"Sasha, Sasha. *Kako si, mali*? How are you, little one?" Zora held his hands as she kept looking at him and repeating the question. And Sasha looked back, smiling, but he didn't say a word.

"*Kak ti malchik moy*? How are you, my little boy?" Tolya said in the Russian he always used. And Sasha sat back on his bed and smiled but still said nothing.

Just as they started getting concerned, a nurse in blue and white walked into the room with a stethoscope around her neck. Middle-aged, with dark hair curled around her head, she looked like someone who had eaten a lot of pasta in her life. She leaned in over Sasha's chest and said, "*Come vai, piccolino*? How are you, little one?" In Italian, of course.

"*Sto bene. Vado a casa!*" Sasha suddenly jabbered away in Italian. Zora knew enough of the language by then to understand he had said he felt good and was ready to go home. She and Tolya just stared at each other in horror as the nurse walked out of the room.

"*Bozhe moy*. Dear God," muttered Tolya. "*Zabyl*. He's forgotten. Forgotten to speak *po nashemu*, in our way."

"*Prokleti Italiani*," cursed Zora. But it was said slowly and quietly while she stared blankly at the wall in front of her as if reading the title of a book she hadn't seen in a long time, rather than cursing the people who made her son forget his native languages.

It was the first and last time Tolya was ever to hear his wife swear. And then he realized she wasn't swearing so much as repeating a mantra she had grown up with—the very words her mother used when describing Mussolini's takeover of their Istrian home.

When Sasha had first gotten sick and was then diagnosed with the flu after surgery, it made sense that the medical reaction was swift. There had been a major flu epidemic throughout the world earlier that year. Even the Pope and the King of Belgium had reportedly come down with it, so everyone understood the initial need for the isolation ward. There was no way Zora would want her son's illness taken lightly. But now Sasha was clearly healthy, and he was still locked away.

"Tolya, I keep having nightmares about Sasha," Zora had told Tolya, more than once. He knew she was remembering that her own mother lost two sons to the flu epidemic of 1918, during the First World War. They too, were living in exile, in a camp. They too, were controlled by foreigners who spoke a different language. And they never came home from that isolation ward.

And in the camps there was now talk that people were being held in the hospital longer than needed. The rumors were that the Italians got paid more for a refugee in the hospital than a refugee in the Campo. It made perfect sense in a macabre sort of way. It had been over two months already, and Tolya realized they had to act, and act at once.

Now, Tolya reached for the blanket and wrapped my brother's long thin body in it, then hugged him close, as he had when Sasha was an infant. He boldly strode down the corridor as if their son had been formally released. He and Mama held their breath as they slipped through the busy entryway and out the front door of the hospital to the bus stop.

He held Sasha close until they were safe in their cubicle in Campo and Zora had soup steaming in front of their son, as she started the process of fattening him back to health.

Shura and Galya leaving the refugee camp at the end of 1952.
Galya in the center with flowers, Zora above her and Babusya to
her left. Shura on the far right and Tolya with his Leica camera
on the left. Their leaving was the last straw for Zora, who then
insisted that Babusya go to France.

CHAPTER TWENTY-FOUR

Zora's ultimatum

Sasha relearned his languages swiftly, but for Zora the whole hospital experience was the final indignity.

"Tolya, I can't take this anymore," she said one day soon after. "Almost everyone else is gone. Your brothers have left: Kolya for Canada, Shura for San Francisco. The Karsanidis are in New York, the Shestakovs in Venezuela. We need to get out of here and move on to the rest of our lives. We've been here almost four years now. It was supposed to be just for a few months, until we got our papers."

"I know, Zora, I know," Tolya replied. They were alone for a change and could talk seriously. Their neighbors had gone to the coffee shop up the road which they could now visit as the rules were easing slightly with the passage of time. "But I thought you were determined to go to America. You know what happened to Kolya and Lyolya in Canada."

"I do, Tolya, I certainly do." Tolya's brother and his wife had expatriated to Canada as indentured servants on a farm. It was the only way to get a visa to North America quickly, and they were anxious to move on. Lyolya couldn't bear living in that old rice factory, sleeping on cots in a large drafty open space divided by old blankets. In Canada, however, they had been badly mistreated, and had finally fled, living in secret in Toronto while trying to normalize their situation. "I don't want to go to Canada; I want us to go to America. We need to start new lives, and I want our children to live in peace and freedom."

"But what can I do?" Tolya struggled to be reasonable, but he, too, was near exhaustion. "We've had our names on the list for American visas since we left Belgrade. I never imagined it could take this long. We just have to wait . . ."

"Tolya, I'm at the end of my endurance. I left my family and my country for you, but I can't live here anymore."

"But, Zora . . ."

"No, don't interrupt me. I have to say it. We always wanted a big family, but I've had three abortions since we've been here because we were told the Americans wouldn't take a pregnant woman. Who knows how long it will be before we're settled enough to consider more children?"

"Three abortions?" asked Tolya, astonished and disturbed.

"Yes, three." Zora bowed her head, holding back the tears that came too easily these days.

"When?" He knew she had two. They had been difficult decisions, but everyone knew a pregnant woman would not pass the required medical exam they had every three months while waiting. And how could they bring another child into this insane uncertainty?

"Two months ago. I went to the gypsy woman." Tolya didn't know about this last one; she hadn't wanted to tell him, but it was out now.

"Oh, good lord! *Zolotko*, honey, that's so dangerous! Why didn't you tell me?"

That last abortion was frightening. Zora was afraid there might never be another child, even if their lives ever returned to normal—whatever that might be. She knew for sure she was never having another abortion. It wasn't her Catholic upbringing that was torturing her; it was how badly she had wanted all those babies and how much it hurt to know she might never hold them. But still, she hadn't been able to tell him. She wasn't sure he could deal with any more.

Zora knew the stress was destroying Tolya. He spent his nights tossing and turning; he was losing weight. The English classes were impossible, and he was convinced he would never learn another language. Waving goodbye to his brothers and their wives hurt deeply. Zora simply couldn't add more pressure. But now she had learned something that convinced her that there was an alternative, and she was not backing away.

"We need to get out of here, Tolya, we must get to America. I'm not spending one more Christmas in this camp."

"I know, Zorića. This is all my fault." Tolya looked at the ground. He felt abandoned and alone and his guilt was killing him. "If you had married a Croat, like your father wanted you to, none of this would be happening."

"Oh, *duše*, I didn't want to marry any Croat. I knew it was you from the moment we met. There was no one else for me. And I haven't changed my mind." She so wanted to walk over and hug this man who was everything to her, but she couldn't give in again. "But there is something you're going to have to do."

"What's that?"

"It's about the home for the elderly in France."

"I can't do it," he said, with a pained—almost frightened—look on his face.

"You can't do what?"

"I can't leave my mother behind."

"You don't have to leave her behind." Their neighbors Tama and Sonja had both been too old to get visas, and they went to a home for older Russian émigrés in Cannes, on the south coast of France. It was sponsored and funded by the Tolstoy Foundation and Zhenya had gotten a letter from them the day before. Zora knew they were happy and doing well.

"She doesn't want to go there," said Tolya, knowing what she was thinking.

"Tama says it's on the beach," Zora continued, determined. "They have a view of the sea from their room. The food is French. There's room for Babusya."

"I've tried to get her to go, but she's afraid. She wants to stay with me. She wants to go with us to America."

"Your mother has always been stubborn. She didn't want you to marry me, she hates me because I am not Russian, and now she is ruining our lives!"

"She doesn't hate you; you're exaggerating."

"At first it was because I wasn't Russian. Then she wouldn't move out of the master bedroom in our apartment in Belgrade. And we couldn't move to our own apartment because you didn't want to abandon her."

"I know, I know. But she's my mother."

"She's also your brother's mother, yet he's gone. She puts him on a pedestal, him and his Russian wife, but she lives with us, and it's my life she criticizes. I'm not taking it anymore."

"What do you mean?"

"What I mean is that either your mother goes to France, or I go home to Yugoslavia."

"You can't mean that, *zolotko*."

"Oh, but I do. Zhenya learned when he went to the consulate to get the paperwork for Tama to go to France that they are not taking any more elderly people in the United States directly from here. The quota for the year is full. If we miss this chance, we will soon be on our fifth year here. It's too much." Zora was determined to finish without crying, but it was getting hard. "I am at my wits end. Our children need a home; our lives need to be going somewhere. I can't live in a barracks partition for the rest of my life, with no work and no future. We've spent four years with five people living in three square meters (one hundred square feet). It's enough."

"She'll hate me."

"She'll get over it. It's not the end of the world. When we get to America we can bring her over. The visa quota from France is bigger than from here, I've heard."

"That could just be another myth, like so many other stories have been."

"It might be, but it's not a myth that we aren't making any progress on the list as we are. Either we get on that list as a family of four rather than five, or three of us are going back home."

"You know I couldn't go back there with you."

"I don't know what to believe anymore. I don't *want* to go back to Yugoslavia, but I can't stay here either. Aren't you sick of it?"

"Oh, dear God. I am so sick of it." Tolya put his head in his hands. "If I take one more picture for one more person who is leaving for their future, I might kill myself."

My father had set up a darkroom in that tiny space and used his camera to earn the money need-ed to supplement our diet, to keep reapplying for the visas, to buy fabric for the clothes Zora sewed for all of us.

Zora looked at him and the desperation in his eyes frightened her. He had always been so strong in his need to make sure we could all rely on him. She finally put her arms around him, as if she were the one who towered over him rather than the other way around, and held him as if she could protect him from what he had to face up to.

"Oh, Tolya, Tolya, I'm so glad we are finally being honest with each other."

"Me too, *zolotko*. It's been too long; it's too hard." He held onto her as if he would never let her go, and Zora knew, deep inside, that he could never do so. She was his life. They had each other and nothing else. Tolya couldn't believe that it had come to this; that he had to choose between his mother and his wife.

He loved them both, but he had to tell his mother,
Daria Pavlovna, that she was going to France.

CHAPTER TWENTY-FIVE

Babusya's last stand

Daria Pavlovna Romanov, as she liked to be known, had, if anything, gotten more determined since living in the Campo. She had worn mourning garments since her husband died years ago, but the man she mourned had known, as well as everyone else, that she was the head of their household and had been ever since she had decided he was the one for her in a small village in the middle of Russia. He may have been the son of Don Cossacks, but she was a *Cossachka* and, while not much has been written about that species of woman, this one was proof that they were not to be messed with. But in Zora she had met her match.

Tolya had already tried to talk to her about France, more than once. She wouldn't budge. But now he was caught between his wife and his mother, and he knew how he would choose. Besides, he really believed it was the right decision, even if it meant going against her wishes.

They were alone and he hoped everyone else in the barracks was too busy to listen in.

"Mama, you know we need to talk."

"I knew she was talking to you again. Don't think I don't know what goes on between you."

"Of course we were talking, Mama. She's my wife, you remember. We have to figure out a way to get to America. We can't stay here forever. It's driving us all mad."

"You don't think I'm going mad since Shura and Kolya left? Who do I have to talk to? Do you think that I want to die here?" He could tell she was working herself into a rage.

"None of us is going to die here. And please don't shout." He wished he could reach out to her, comfort her, but she was unbending and unyielding. "I'd do anything I could to take care of you, Mama, but I'm getting older. I'm almost forty. It's time to move on. With every month that goes by, my opportunities to get work in America will get fewer. Shura has written me that he has found work, and I can join him. He's fixing appliances in San Francisco, and that's something I know how to do also."

"Well, I am glad that your future is taken care of, but what about me? Why does everyone assume this is my fault? Why should I go by myself to France to live with all those old people?"

"Mama, Mama, it wouldn't be for a long time, just until we get settled in America. Then we'll get you over to join us. I promise."

"You can't promise me anything. You've been waiting almost four years for those visas, and there's no guarantee you're going to get them."

"Mama, we've been over all this before. I'm filling out the paperwork in the morning, and you will go to France next month. As soon we get to San Francisco, we'll do everything we can to make sure you can join us."

"You know what you can do with trying to get me to join you. If you make me leave now, I will never speak with you or that foreign wife of yours again."

"Please, Mama, don't be like that. The children would miss you."

"The children would miss me? What about you? You're my son."

"Of course I would miss you." He chuckled in spite of himself. Suddenly it felt like he was dealing with his daughter, not his mother. "You're my mother. I know you're not going to abandon me."

"Why don't you just send *her* back home to her country. This is all *her* idea; I know it is. See how *she* would feel about it if it happened to *her*!"

"I don't want to send my wife back anywhere. I'm already worried that she might be thinking about it. Her father's not doing well, you know. Please be reasonable."

"You're not going to get your way with me. Don't think you can sweet talk your way past this. If you send me away, I am not coming to live with you again. You'll just be on your own."

He didn't have the heart to tell her how happy this would most likely make Zora. And probably him too, for that matter. The constant tension was getting old. Zora really tried to get along with her, but Daria Pavlovna just couldn't get over the fact that he didn't marry the young Russian woman she had her eye on for him.

"I'm going to write Shura about this, don't think I won't." She always used Shura, her eldest, when she wanted her way with her other children. But now he was already gone and living in San Francisco.

"I already have written him about it. I don't know why he hasn't replied. But he knows." Privately, Tolya figured Shura was not getting in the middle of this. Always her favorite, he was going to let someone else take the responsibility for the hard choices.

Shura was shrewd; he always landed on his feet. Well, that was just fine with Tolya. Once they got to America, he knew he would be able to count on Shura to help him find work and help them find a home.

"I'm sorry, Mama; you will have to do what you need to do. But I am filling out the paperwork tomorrow."

The family is happy to be finally leaving the refugee camp,
waving to those still left behind.

CHAPTER TWENTY-SIX

Leaving Zhenya

It was the end of 1953 and Zora could hardly believe it might finally be happening. They were heading for the consulate; their visas had come through. There was no longer a need to go to Genoa. The United States now had an office in Trieste. Tolya's mother had left for France a few months earlier. All reports from Zhenya's aunts indicated that things were going fine, but nothing had been heard from her. She was in a sulk, upset that she had been sent away, and swore to anyone who would listen that she would never live with us again. Zora would have heaved a sigh of relief had she believed that was true. Deep inside she somehow knew Babusya would be back. But at that moment, she cared about nothing except getting on a boat to America.

Since the early 1920s, exiled Russians could apply to have help from the Tolstoy Foundation in relocating to another country. Ever since the author's daughter established it after the Russian Revolution, the foundation had helped support a diaspora that spread around the world. In my family, Tolstoy was like a member of the extended family. People talked about his *fond,* the foundation, endlessly.

As time passed, Zora had worried because there were rumors that they were running out of funds. As it turned out, by the time our family was ready to leave, in late 1953, the *fond* could no longer grant the money for transportation, but they would loan enough money to cover the cost of passage. Zora and Tolya were grateful for the support, as they had no ability to pay for the trip after four years in the camp. Tolya made some money with his photographic work, but not enough to feed them. Whatever funds they had brought with them from Yugoslavia four years earlier had been spent on living.

Everything happened very quickly after the visas were approved. We qualified for a loan for third class passage and received the funds. It seemed my parents were going into Trieste on a daily basis. They learned the schedule for overnight trains to Genoa by heart. And then they heard that an American ship, the *SS Constitution,* was leaving for New York at the end of December. They planned to go buy tickets the next day.

Sasha caught a cold that day, so Mama stayed home with us. We could not afford to have anyone sick before everything was finalized. There were many horror stories about someone who was not allowed into America because they got ill on the ship going over. Mama was taking no chances, especially with Sasha's previous experience in the hospital. Tolya signed out of camp, walked up to the road and took the tram into town.

It seemed to take forever, but finally Mama saw him walking back down the road.

She had been waiting for him at the front gate, sitting with Zhenya and me and talking. Actually, the two of us were talking. Mama was just counting the minutes, waiting to learn what had happened at the shipping-line offices. "Were you able to get the tickets?" she called as he walked up to the gate.

"We have four third class tickets from Genoa to New York leaving December 23!" Tolya beamed from ear to ear. He hadn't been this relaxed and happy in years.

"And I got a letter from the Karsanidis today," Zora replied with a smile. Our first friends in the Campo, the Karsanidis had left two years earlier and had settled down in Manhattan. "They say we can stay with them when we get to New York."

"That's wonderful, *zolotko*. I am afraid the tickets cost much more than we planned. We will have almost nothing left over after the voyage, so it's a good thing we won't have to pay for a hotel."

"Oh, Tolya. Right now I am so happy. I probably wouldn't care if we had nothing left over. I know we can start a new life."

They hugged and walked over to where Zhenya and I were still sitting talking. They weren't sure I understood what was happening.

"Zhenya, Tania, we're going to America!"

"Oh, thank God. I am so happy for you." Zhenya beamed. "You will love it there, Tania!"

"Isn't Uncle Zhenya coming with us?" I asked.

"Not right away, Tania. He and Auntie Vava will be coming soon though."

"I don't want to go without Zhenya and Vava," said I, starting to sob and burrowing my head in the old man's jacket.

"We'll be there soon, *dorogaya*, dear one," Zhenya said. "You'll be with your mama and papa and your brother Sasha. Of course you want to go."

"I don't! I don't! I want to stay with you."

"*Taniusha*. We want you to come with us." My father tried to cuddle me, but I was too frightened of what was happening and just kept sobbing and holding on to Zhenya, as if he were my lifeline.

Mama knew I would be heartbroken to leave my dearest friends. Even she had a hard time imagining life without them. She and I would have to develop a new relationship. I think Mama knew somewhere deep inside that she had neglected me over the years. But she also knew I was always loved and cared for by everyone around her. She would make it up to me once we were in America.

"Tania," she said, "Vava gave me one of her old winter coats, and I used it to make a little warm coat for you to wear when we get to America. Come with me, and we can try it on."

"No! No." I stomped my foot on the ground. "I want Zhenya to come with me. I don't care about a coat."

Mama was afraid it was going to be a long trip, with just the four of us. But she was confident that once we were on our way I too would start looking forward to our new life.

"Never mind about the coat. Let's go tell Sasha the news!"

"Oh, all right." I always loved having news for Sasha. I jumped up and ran toward the barracks.

Zora and the children on the deck of the ship getting ready to
leave Genoa, December 1953

Ship manifest of *SS Constitution* sailing from Genoa to New York December 1953. Four stateless passengers who had waited years for this trip.

List of Passengers

Tourist Class

Sailing from Naples
Sunday the 20th of December 1953

to

New York via Genoa, Cannes and Gibraltar

SS Constitution.

CHAPTER TWENTY-SEVEN

The *SS Constitution*

In December of 1953, by the time we left, most of our family and friends had already gone to America. Those who were still in Campo San Sabba came with us to the train station in Trieste to see us off. I wore the coat Mama had made from the small piece of creamy wool that had once been an old coat of Vava's. I had a felt hat with a round brim. In the photos someone took with my father's camera, I looked scared, excited and sad at the same time.

I clung to Uncle Zhenya, my favorite person in the whole world, the grandfather in place of the one I never knew. He and Aunt Vava were still waiting for their visas. Everyone kept telling me they would join us in America, but at the last moment I didn't want to let him go.

"Don't cry, *Tanichka*; we'll be there soon," he said, breaking up in tears. "You'll see your Uncle Shura and Aunt Galya when you get to America. And we'll be there soon; you'll see." I rubbed my face against his. I had never seen Uncle Zhenya cry. His tears mingled with mine and ran down into my mouth. They were warm.

At that point, he passed me to my tall, handsome papa, who lifted me high above the group of well-wishers and carried me, repeating soothing phrases while I continued sobbing, into the train car. I wanted to stop crying, but it was hard. People had been leaving for America for my entire life, and now it was our turn. I had always been excited when people talked about going to America, but now I wasn't so sure I'd be happy there. I did not understand why we had to leave anyone behind. And what if I didn't like America?

Our bags had been packed for days. Our clothing fit in a few small, brown suitcases. One larger orange pigskin *kufer*, or trunk, squared off and with a large handle, held the special clothes brought from Yugoslavia when we first came. At that time, Mama and Papa had heard from friends that American ladies valued things made by hand. They bought lovely embroidered voile blouses, pretty hand-stitched dresses for little girls, and embroidered tablecloths and napkins. We didn't know that this had all gone out of style while we waited in the camp. Not a single piece ever got sold. After we got to America my mother realized this and decided I could wear those little dresses, but I was too embarrassed to do so.

But as we left Trieste, those articles were carefully stowed and the train pulled away into the night. All four of us leaned out the window and waved wildly. In those pictures, too, I think you could see the traces of tears on my face even though I was beaming.

We had been to Genoa once before, when my Aunt Galya and Uncle Shura left for America on the same ship, and we went to resubmit our paperwork and prove our identities. The beautiful park on the hillside and the docks were familiar to me, and I knew what the ship would look like. Once we were there, I could hardly bear to wait any longer. Finally, it was time to board.

The small stateroom seemed enormous to me after the cramped rooms in the camp. It didn't take much to seem like luxury. After years of sharing two small cots for all four of us, it was a thrill to be in a room with a bed that felt nearly the size of our whole sleeping area in the barracks. We could all fit on it, and it was our first experience of snuggling together in bed with Mama and Papa. After we got to America we spent all our Sunday mornings in our parents' bed, drinking *Turska kafa*, Turkish coffee, and hot chocolate and talking.

The ship was American. It was our introduction to America, really, and we were crossing during Christmas week. The crew was very nice and they smiled a lot, but I couldn't understand anything they said. There was a big tree, and they had presents for us. Mine was a long-legged teddy bear, and I loved it. No one had ever given me a present like that before. Mama told me I could keep it when we got off the ship, but I still worried that it was only for the ship. It slept under my pillow when I left the stateroom.

The second morning of the trip, Mama had gone out to get a cup of coffee while we were still asleep, but suddenly she rushed back in to wake us.

"Tania, get up. Sasha, dress quickly. There's a surprise outside!" she cried gaily, while pulling up warm tights and tying shoelaces. I hadn't heard Mama shouting happily like that in a long time. Maybe I had never heard her sound like that, and I was really excited for the treat.

We ran up the stairs and found the decks full of people shouting, laughing, catching things that seemed to be flying through the air. Papa lifted me high in the air and carried me toward the railing. Mama and Sasha followed us.

The ship seemed to be standing still in the water, and near it were some big cliffs with white houses and a big fort. We were surrounded by what Papa called a *flotilla*—lots of little boats of all kinds. People were tossing coins to the people in the boats, and they were throwing back brightly colored things.

"Papa, can we get something?" I asked. I was almost frightened by the colors, the noise, and the confusion. But everyone was laughing, so I started jumping up and down on his shoulders and clapping my hands. Papa put me down so I wouldn't jump off the boat by accident.

"What would you like?" he asked. Then he put his head near Sasha and me, and smiled. "Shall we get Mama a scarf?" he asked, conspiratorially.

"Papa, look! That man is pointing toward us," cried Sasha. "And he has pretty scarves. Let's get one of those for Mama!"

Papa shouted some words that I didn't understand in some strange language. The man shouted back, they laughed, and then Papa said "*Si, Señor!*" He pulled some coins out of his pocket and wrapped them in his handkerchief, then tossed them. I was worried that the coins would land in the sea. But the man in the boat caught them. Then he wrapped the scarf up in Papa's handkerchief and threw it back. It came sailing through the sky toward us, and Papa caught it.

It was gorgeous. Huge and colored in bright blues, reds and greens, it had pictures of the city and fort all over it. It turned out we were at a place called the Rock of Gibraltar. It was the end, Papa said, of the calm seas and the beginning of the Atlantic Ocean, and America was on the other side. And we had a souvenir to take to America with us, a beautiful scarf that Mama wore for many years under her coat when she went downtown.

Then the ship pulled out into the ocean, and we went down for breakfast. We had a table to ourselves in a big, gaily decorated room. There were lots of spoons and forks and plates and glasses on the table. People speaking English came by to ask what we wanted. My parents spoke a little English, a lot more than Sasha and I did. At first I was unhappy because no one understood me. Soon, however, I felt very important, being served by kind, smiling strangers. I had never seen so many people who smiled so much, even though they didn't know you. In the camps, hardly anyone smiled—except Vava and Zhenya, of course.

"Tania, do you want an egg?" Mama asked.

"No, no egg. I want some of that!" I cried, pointing to a brightly colored box that had a picture of a cartoon animal on it. It was my first taste of American cereal. It was kind of sweet—I wasn't sure I liked it.

Sasha ordered a boiled egg, and it came in something else I had never seen: a small cup that was no bigger than half the egg. The waiter sliced the top off the egg in one swift stroke. He then offered to sprinkle the egg from something in his hand that looked like a tiny bowl of sugar. Sasha said "yes," and the waiter sprinkled the white powder over the soft egg.

"Why is he putting that on Sasha's egg?" I asked.

"It will make it taste better," Mama replied.

"Then I want some in my cocoa," I said.

"But Tania, that's salt!" Mama said.

"I don't care what it is; I want some."

"*Zolotko*, it won't taste good," Papa tried.

"Yes, it will. Sasha got some, and I want some. I know it will make my cocoa taste better." It seemed all my life Sasha got the good things, and I was considered too young to have them.

I am not sure why, but my parents gave in. The incredulous waiter, having understood none of this, finally poured a tiny amount of the white powder into my cocoa.

The cocoa, of course, was ruined. I bravely sipped at it, pretending it was fine.

The ship meanwhile, had started listing more dramatically than in the calm Mediterranean. Shortly after breakfast, I got violently ill, and stayed sick to my stomach for most of the journey to New York.

I suspect I was seasick, but Mama told me it was because I had that salt in my cocoa. I was angry that she never took my side, but perversely it only made me more stubborn and determined to make my own choices rather than listen to her.

Fortunately, I recovered in time to stand on the deck with the others, watching and waiting to see something called the Statue of Liberty. But heavy clouds closed in and we saw nothing. Ellis Island had been closed for some time, the flood of immigrants to America had slowed, and our immigration processing, Mama told me later, was almost anticlimactic. All those years of worrying, and then some man in a uniform just looked at our documents, stamped them, and without any emotion waved his hand so the next people in line could be checked. The disembarkation was a blur of activity, and then we set off to find our friends the Karsanidis, who had moved to New York from the Campo.

Papa and Mama walked to a taxi. It was yellow with a big sign on top, and as easy to find as the Karsanidis had described in their letter. Mama swore she could have said the address in English — she had practiced on the ship — but Papa had a piece of paper that he gave to the driver and we took off.

America was not very nice.

It was cold and gray, and the taxi windows kept getting foggy so we couldn't see much. There were lots of people on the streets, but they were all moving as if they were in a big hurry. Everywhere we looked there were big buildings. You couldn't see the sky. We had waited all those years for this?

Finally the driver found the building with the right numbers on it. It was very tall and dirty. We climbed long flights in a hot stairwell and walked through halls that reeked of boiled cabbage and garlic. Sasha and I gagged and made faces at each other.

We had often discussed where we would live in America, and my mother always promised we would decide together.

"Mama, we don't want to live here," Sasha said, before they even asked. He knew he was speaking for me too. "We want to go to San Francisco and live with Uncle Shura!"

"So, you've already decided?" laughed my father.

"I hate New York; it stinks here!" Sasha said. I added, "I thought America would be pretty and warm, not cold and smelly like this. Please, let's go to San Francisco."

"Not all of New York can be like this," Papa said, unconvincingly. "And San Francisco could be worse. What do you think, Zora?"

"We told the children they could decide." Mama said. "Are you two sure that's what you want? It's an important decision, you know. We can't come back if you don't like it."

"We are, we are," we both shouted. "San Francisco, San Francisco, we're going to San Francisco!"

"Well, it's been a long time since we could choose where we live," Mama said, getting teary. "I think we should do what you want. We want you to like living in America."

We had no idea what San Francisco was, but by now it seemed magical compared to this place, this New York, that we had instantly hated. It was dirty and dark on the sidewalks, hot in the stairways and stinky in the long narrow hallways. Our friends were nice, but they couldn't make up for all this. We just kept jumping up and down and shouting until Papa interrupted.

"Well, now that you have made up your minds, come with me." Papa took us to the nearby station to buy tickets.

The very next day we set off on a four-day-and-night trip on a Greyhound bus bound for San Francisco.

That evening, as my mother was bundling me up to go to sleep in my window seat, Papa suddenly shouted, *"Smotrite! Taniusha! Sashura! Sneg*! Look! Taniusha, Sashura! Snow!"

As we stared out at the twilight, the bus driver announced we were approaching Philadelphia. The bus slowed down, and a small country church caught my eye. The first snow I had ever seen fell gently around its steepled roof in a halo. I gasped with pleasure, and smiled, contentedly, as I fell asleep.

We had made the right choice after all. America *was* beautiful!

The four unit house owned by Tolya and his brother Shura in San Francisco in 1956. Zora and Galya are in the window, Tania and Sasha are with their uncle Shura on the street.

CHAPTER TWENTY-EIGHT

San Francisco, home

The Russian community in San Francisco welcomed us. Our sponsors were Shura and Galya. The family of Alex Akalovsky, who was later to serve as Nixon's translator in Russia, had sponsored them, and in return Mama and Papa sponsored later arrivals. We all crowded into friends' apartments, illegally, at some risk of being evicted.

The city was struggling, as many were in those days of emerging suburbia, and we arrived as it neared bottom. Market Street merchants watched their business collapse and *downtown* deteriorated to a dirty word. The Crystal Palace, a venerable food emporium, gasped a last breath. The ornate and elegant Fox Theater was razed with only minor debate. Cable cars were threatened, and a freeway covered half the waterfront before being stopped dead, half built, by protests.

There were actually plans in place to dump fill into the Bay and build houses there; much of the bay was lost to farms and developments like Foster City before sanity was regained—thanks to three women in Berkeley and the Save the Bay movement. The inner city rotted, rents tumbled, buildings deteriorated. Many years later San Francisco Victorians regained their cachet, but in the meantime many were replaced by something called "urban renewal" and "housing projects."

Meanwhile, values sank in many once vibrant neighborhoods. After the initial months of crowding in with friends, we finally moved into an apartment of our own. My father and Uncle Shura both worked for the Sunbeam Corporation, fixing small appliances. Somehow they quickly saved the minimum down payment required to buy a run-down building on Hayes Street near Golden Gate Park. It had become an inner city neighborhood that people fled for the suburbs. The old Lowell High School was just blocks away, but it was soon shuttered and relocated at the outer edge of the city where Stonestown—the first shopping mall—was also built at the time.

Old homes were being torn down and Tolya and Shura hauled home abandoned windows, appliances, and hardwood flooring. They rebuilt and painted. Sand from the beach was bagged—at night, to avoid detection—and a giant sandbox for me and Sasha appeared in the backyard. Aunt Galya's mother and her husband eventually ended up living in one of the apartments, and I was beside myself with joy when Uncle Zhenya and Vava moved in next to us.

When my grandmother arrived a year or two later, she was squeezed onto a couch in the living room. As far as I know, no one ever mentioned the fact that she had sworn never to talk to my mother or father again after they made her go to France.

Her personality hadn't shifted much. She took me to the park every day, but she doted on Sasha—the oldest boy. One evening she snuck into the room Sasha and I slept in—until he got tired of my bedwetting and moved into the dining room—and handed Sasha a dime. She then turned to me and said, "*A tyebe nichevo*. And for you, nothing." Sasha shared it with me, as he did everything she gave him, but it made me determined that the world was not going to look down on me just because I was a female. Once planted, that chip on my shoulder just grew bigger.

Even though I loved being close to Zhenya and Vava and the rest of them, I eventually grew to hate being foreign. I loved my family; I just wished they were more American.

I had Russian girlfriends from Russian School and Russian Scouts, but I wanted to be more like the American girls. Every day, I went to what other people thought of as school. At our house the local public school, Andrew Jackson, a block away, was called American School.

I didn't know what the homes of the little American girls were like, but I was pretty sure they were different from ours. They didn't wear homemade dresses, and their lunch boxes didn't have homemade pickles and homemade *tortes*. I was pretty sure their mothers weren't making jams and canning grilled peppers. And people spoke American where they lived.

I didn't dream about being rich, I dreamed of getting dresses from J.C. Penney's. Most of all, I wanted a store-bought cake for my birthday. Not the kind of cake that Zora produced from wonderful natural ingredients. No. I wanted the kind of cake that shared shelf space with Wonder Bread, the kind that was covered with a pure white butter cream and topped with red roses. The kind that I knew all the little American girls in my class ate on their birthdays.

My desire had nothing to do with taste and everything to do with fitting in. But there was no easy way to bring up this secret desire at home. Papa once told me his taste buds sang arias to the tastes and aromas of Mama's kitchen.

I liked being there well enough. Special things from Mama's baking spread everywhere: chocolate-covered spoons that I got to lick clean; vanilla beans ground into powder and mixed with sugar for chocolate *tortes*; cooling hazelnuts that had been gently roasted; gentle currents of warm air emerging from the oven door.

One day I sat on my green vinyl chair at the Formica table. The smell of coffee beans roasting rose from the black iron contraption Papa had built from a frying pan. It sat on the flame and required attention the entire time of the roasting, to avoid burning the beans. Papa was the one roasting that day, but he was taking a break, probably for a cigarette out on the back stairwell.

Suddenly, clouds of smoke came pouring through the small opening in the top of the pan, accompanied by the acrid stench of burning. In an instant the normal womb-like comfort of the kitchen vanished.

Before I had time to get too frightened, my mother ran in from her sewing room and took over. The house didn't burn down, but Papa was evicted from the kitchen — Mama's kitchen, where he was just a visitor. She grabbed the *jezva*, the same old Turkish coffee pot that was used in all her homes back in Yugoslavia. Babusya wandered in and reached for the traditional tall elaborately etched brass tube that she used to grind the coffee.

"Mama, why do you roast your own coffee?" I asked, wondering why everything we did had to be so different from other people.

"Well, you know, I can't find the right kind of beans in any store," she said.

"What about the Armenian on Clement?" I asked. We referred to all shopkeepers by nationality and location in our house, and no one ever became confused about which one was being discussed.

"Oh no, his are not even close. I think he makes it for American tastes; it doesn't have any body to it," Zora responded. She considered anything for "American" tastes bland, heavy, and full of artificial flavors. "The one on Polk is the closest, but roasting our own is the only sure way of getting it perfect. If your father doesn't forget about it, that is." She smiled.

"What about getting an electric coffee grinder?" Since my father repaired appliances for Sunbeam, our kitchen was festooned with the most exotic reconstructed devices. We even had an electric egg cooker in case anyone didn't know how to boil an egg.

"We had one of those grinders for a while; but it's not as good as doing it by hand. The beans heat up from being rotated at high speeds, and the knives smash them all together. It's just not the same." She effortlessly executed the six other things she was doing in the kitchen while I vaguely pretended to do homework. "Besides, Babusya likes grinding the coffee."

Babusya just chuckled to herself and kept grinding.

In those days Maxwell House or Folger's medium roast pre-ground coffee was being percolated to death in most American kitchens. In our house, the coffee making was a ceremony, the drinking a rite.

"Can I make the coffee?" I asked. I'd seen it done a dozen times a day; I could make it in my sleep.

"Yes, but be careful. Don't burn yourself."

The water in the *jezva* boiled. I poured off a little bit into a small Turkish coffee cup. To the water remaining in the *jezva*, I added five big scoops of the fine black powder, stirring it in carefully. The coffee heated to a boil, then slowly rose toward the top of the *jezva*. Just before it overflowed, I swished it away from the heat to let it settle back down. I did this three times altogether, stirring it to set the flavor. A lovely brown crown of foam formed over the top. After the third time, I poured the water reserved earlier back into the *jezva*. This helped the grounds, which remained in the coffee, to settle.

The aroma now filled the apartment, and Papa wandered back just in time to see the coffee being poured. Uncle Shura showed up at the back door, coming down from his upstairs apartment. With Babusya, they settled into a nice Saturday afternoon chat. No one asked why my Aunt Galya hadn't come down. We knew she was busy in her kitchen, cooking and baking, just like Mama.

As the coffee event got underway, Vava and Zhenya somehow got wind of it and showed up, coming from their apartment in the compound. We'd left enough coffee in the *jezva* for two more tiny Turkish coffee cups. Once the coffee was poured, they deliberately stirred in the sugar, then let it sit until the grounds settled to the bottom. They knew you didn't drink it all, just the right amount to avoid getting the grounds in your mouth with the last sip.

Vava, like the gypsy everyone believed she was, wanted to read everyone's future in the remaining coffee grounds. We turned the used cups upside down, and when they set up Vava started her tales.

"There is some violence in your future," she said to my grandmother in a mysterious tone. "See how these currents are competing with each other? Here and here."

My brother just laughed to himself, but I looked at the cup. Sure enough, the jagged edges seemed violent. Instead of rolling around like the normal single Rorschach blot, her wet grounds had spattered, and then dripped over each other in a confusing melee. Babusya just laughed, and then realized it was time to go watch TV: Saturday afternoon wrestling, her favorite show, was about to air! We chuckled at the reference to violence and at this ungrandmotherly activity of Babusya's.

One day I had finally pestered Mama enough and she brought home a store-bought white cake with red roses for my birthday. Everyone took a small bite and left the rest on their plate, finding it completely inedible. I took a large piece, savoring every sweet bite. I even got to eat all the rest of the roses after the family left. Of course, I got terribly sick to my stomach from the American cake.

I really had to surrender. Having a life that resembled anything going on in my friends' homes just wasn't going to happen.

CHAPTER TWENTY-NINE

Speak Serbian, Tania

One evening when I was a teenager I sat in my family dining room while my parents entertained a group of visitors. The conversation swirled around me. Rather than our usual friends who all spoke Russian, these people were speaking *po našemu*. I understood every word they said. But when I opened my mouth to respond, nothing came out. Nothing. I stared at them, open-mouthed, and said not one word. They assumed I didn't speak their language. Perhaps I had forgotten it even if I spoke it at one time?

What was going on? I wondered. *Was this a dream? Or, more accurately, a nightmare?*

I always spoke different languages with my father and with my mother. That's just how it worked.

He was Papa, and he and I spoke his language—
Russian—and she was Mama, and we spoke in her
language—Serbo-Croatian, as it was then called. It
was true in the refugee camp, and it continued in
America. I don't remember what language I used
with my brother when I first learned to talk. Once
we learned English, Sasha became Alex, and we
spoke English exclusively to each other.

Russian and Serbo-Croatian are both Slavic languages, so they have some similarity, but they are
different enough that a speaker of one would not
understand the other.

In San Francisco, we lived in a virtual Russian
community, although not that many Russians lived
in our physical neighborhood. The only place we
spoke English was in American School.

All our parents' friends, and ours, were Russian.
We attended Russian School after American public
school and on Saturdays. We prayed in a Russian
Orthodox Church, joined the Russian Scouts, sang
Russian songs and learned Russian poems. We were
punished for speaking English in any of those set-
tings.

I had learned Serbo-Croatian long after we had left
Yugoslavia, so I had never lived anywhere that people used the language. And the only place I had ever
spoken Serbo-Croatian was at home with Mama. Un-

like Russian, no one ever forced me to say a word in my mother's language, but I always spoke it fluently and felt comfortable in it.

So I spoke this language with exactly one person in my life. I have never even heard of a similar circumstance, even in bilingual families — but I never thought about it much. It was just what I did.

I never studied the language in school, but I could read and write in it for one simple reason. Serbo-Croatian is a true phonetic language. It is spelled exactly as it sounds. Since I studied Russian and English in their respective schools, I knew both the Cyrillic and the Latin alphabets. Serbian is written in Cyrillic and Croatian in Latin. I could handle both.

It's an almost bizarre notion for an English speaker, where phonetics is a challenging concept and spelling is an art, not a science. Simple examples abound. The letter combinations *I* and *eye* share the same sound, as do *be* and *bee*; *to* and *too* and *two*; *wear* and *where* and *ware*. The whole notion of phonetics in English is comical, but in Serbo-Croatian it really works.

I lived in this purportedly American world of Russians with a single Yugoslav interloper — my mother — into my teens. And then in the 1960s, the political situation in Yugoslavia started loosening up, and various cultural groups started showing up in San Francisco. One time a Serbian *Kolo*, or dance group came to perform in the city. Through our dear friend, Anatol Joukowsky, a dance professor at San Francisco State and once head of the Belgrade Ballet, they came to our house for dinner.

They were a noisy, jovial group, and my mother cooked up one of her delicious meals. My father served *rakija* or *slivovitz*, the national Yugoslavian drink. Sasha and I sat, mostly listening.

As my mother stepped into the kitchen between courses, one of the young men turned to me.

"So your father says you understand our language. Do you have many Serbian friends, did you study it at school?"

"No, I …"

Suddenly I was tongue-tied. No words emerged from my mouth. My brain froze. I looked at the young man. I looked at my father. They smiled, stared at me.

Nothing would come from my mouth.

"Maybe she doesn't speak *po našemu*, in our way," said the young woman sitting next to him, trying to get me off the hot seat.

"Of course she does," said my father, smiling at me in a puzzled fashion.

And I just continued to sit, mute, growing more embarrassed by the moment. This was surely a nightmare.

Suddenly the door from the kitchen swung open, my mother entered the room with the platter of *sarme*, stuffed cabbage leaves. She said, "What's wrong?" and my mind freed instantly, and I spoke, freely and fluently, *po našemu*.

Everyone just sat and stared at us.

And then it hit me. For the first time in my life I needed to speak Serbo-Croatian with someone other than my mother, and I couldn't do it. I had a single-person language, and I had to be physically looking at Mama to speak it. I didn't even know anyone other than Mama who used that language, and my mind refused to divulge the secrets of that private tongue to anyone else. It was truly my "mother tongue" — but in a very unique way.

For all those years, my mother and I had existed in a cocoon whose wrapping was a unique language — the language of a country I was born in but left long before I learned to talk. It was many years before I understood just how important her gift of language would turn out to be for our relationship.

Tania and the Greg, Christmas 1969.

CHAPTER THIRTY
The Greg

When I was young, my yearning to be more like the American girls was strong. I envied them their roots in this country, the fact that their grandmothers could speak English. But it was a remote issue, as they existed in a world separate from ours.

By junior high we lived in a nice neighborhood and I started visiting American friends at their homes. But I was embarrassed to bring them home, lest they find out how "different" I was. As for boys, until high school, I'd only had crushes on or dated Russian boys. I hardly knew anyone else.

But when I was in the eleventh grade, I briefly played on the George Washington High School tennis team, and I met a tennis player out at the Golden Gate Park tennis courts. He was tall, handsome, charming, and, of course, American.

Here's the rub. Because I was only five when we came to this country, even though it was my third language, I spoke English like any other American girl. I had no accent.

I was 5'4", weighed about 115 pounds, had brownish blond hair, dark brown eyes, a light complexion that tanned easily, and I looked and sounded like any other California girl.

So there was no reason, when the tall handsome tennis player asked me out, that he would have any idea of what my saying a simple "yes" entailed. It wasn't that I kept the fact that my parents were foreign a secret. I just didn't think or talk about it a lot—until he came over to pick me up, that is.

Mama learned English much faster than my father did. She was more outgoing and less self-conscious. But she always had trouble with a few of the less logical parts of English grammar. Take the definite article; the word THE. *The* door. *The* car. Turn on *the* light. In her language, as in all Slavic languages, this word does not exist.

"I am in the house" sounds better than "I am in house" because our ear is used to it, but both are perfectly clear. We say "I am going to the hospital," but the British say "I am going to hospital" and no one is confused. And, of course, proper names don't require the definite article. In fact, they sound bizarre with one unless they are part of a modifier. For example, we say "I read *King Lear*," but "I read *the* King James Bible."

Now, none of this is confusing to me or any other native English speaker — it's intuitive. But you could understand that it might be challenging for a non-native speaker.

Having gone through mortifying missteps that included Mama requesting sheets as 'shits' at JC Penney, and sending beer to school with my brother in the third grade when root beer was called for, I wanted to be sure Mama was prepped for the big event — my first American date.

"Mama, his name is Greg."

"Greg?" she asked, as if I had said some particularly challenging word, a name that had landed off the moon.

"Greg," I repeated.

"Greg." She rolled it around in her mouth, practiced it a few times. It had that middle European heavy rolled 'r'; the short 'e' was crisp and came from the top of her mouth rather than the full-cheeked version he would be used to, but it would do. She wrote it down to practice later. For her, it was much harder to remember than, say, Miloslav, or Vladimir, or Slobodan.

So I wanted to rehearse his arrival.

"When he comes, I'll be upstairs. Just call up and tell me he's here, Okay?"

"Tania, enough. I wasn't born in a barn, you know. Go get dressed."

She wanted me to look pretty. She wished I would wear a dress she had made for me, comb my hair, put on some lipstick. I wanted to look like a flower child of San Francisco in 1965 — in old tattered clothes, or even jeans. It killed her every time I left the house looking like someone whose mother couldn't afford nice clothes.

We were both suffering the disease of non-acceptance, but somehow we toiled on.

I pushed her out of my bedroom. She went downstairs. I considered going and opening the door myself, but something kept me back. Besides, it was too late. The doorbell rang.

I was in the upstairs hallway, where Sasha and I used to sit, legs through the rungs, listening to our parents' parties downstairs, with the bawdy singing getting louder as the vodka flowed more freely.

I heard the faucet in the kitchen turn off. I felt her wiping her hands, taking her apron off, heading for the front door.

She opened the door and said, "Hello, won't you come in?"

Then he said something, and she replied, "I'm the mother."

I cringed, heard no response; what could he say? He stepped in; she closed the door, turned toward the stairs, and called to me, in a proud voice, "Tania, the Greg is here!"

The family in San Francisco in 1977, when Alex was completing his PhD in neuro-physiological psychology at UCSF medical school and Tania was at the Graduate School of Business at Stanford.

MINNESOTA BUSINESS JOURNAL

The State of High Tech
What the Experts Think

Minnesota's Fastest-Growing High-Tech Companies

Why Banks Say "No"

Tania as the CEO of a computer software company in
Minneapolis, Minnesota, 1985.

CHAPTER THIRTY-ONE
Life in America

Mama and I survived each other, although it was never easy. Over the succeeding years I lived out a rags to riches immigrant story, adapted for an insanely determined female. *Someday,* I thought, *I'll write a book about it.*

I attended the decaying San Francisco public school system, working a part-time job in the best delicatessen in the city.

Of course there's a Zora backstory to this. Mama shopped at Petrini Plaza for years. It had the best meat department after the Crystal Palace on Market closed, and she was very careful to buy only the best. The store was in a neighborhood, near the old Lowell High School, that had seen better days. Wealthy society ladies drove in from Pacific Heights, but the neighborhood women were either poor blacks or immigrants, and the mix created an amazing synchronicity. The more steaks and roasts one group bought, the more offal—brains, kidneys, hearts, tripe, tongues, pancreas (sweetbreads), and other innards—there were to be gotten rid of. These items, which I mostly detested, were the beloved ingredients of Mama's favorite dishes. And the butchers would basically give them away. She was such a regular that both Sasha and I were eventually given jobs in the delicatessen—Maison Gourmet. Sasha decided stringing raw chickens in a cooler was not for him, but I worked the front counter until I graduated from college. I was hired before I was fifteen, paid illegally as "supplies" until my sixteenth birthday, and on that day joined Butcher's Union Local 101. Since Sundays led to double pay at union rates, I made more on an hourly basis there than I did in my first professional job after graduating from one of the best universities in the country. I can still probably find that union card somewhere.

I received a scholarship to college through the Ford Fund because my father was employed at Philco, an engineering company that Ford bought. I studied math at Berkeley in the late 1960s, to the accompaniment of the Free Speech Movement, People's Park, and Vietnam War protests. My parents, like most people fleeing communism, voted staunchly conservative and Berkeley in the 1960s was the antithesis of everything they believed in. But for me, it embodied a key step in my ongoing fight for self-determination, and it propelled me far away from my roots in the San Francisco Russian community. My fierce independence continued unabated, and I always worked two or three jobs and lived on my own, so I had no financial obligations to my family and no one could criticize what I did or how I thought. At least I could choose not to listen when they insisted on doing so.

I graduated from Berkeley while on strike in 1970, outraged that the United States had bombed Cambodia. The entire math department protested, and our graduation ceremony was actually cancelled. Interestingly, by the time the ceremony was reenacted for us, in 1990, I was a business executive serving on an advisory board of the college. Somehow protest had morphed into success.

"The Greg" and I broke up just weeks before our planned wedding, shortly after my college graduation. Instead, I moved on to a successful career in the computer business, which was just getting rolling in those days. I lived in France for a few years, them moved to Minnesota for an irresistible promotion. While spending the next decade in the Midwest, I took enough time out in California to earn a graduate degree from the Stanford Graduate School of

Business. I also met my future husband, Harold, who had also attended the Stanford GSB, and had moved to Minnesota after he finished. With our marriage, I gained two stepchildren who fortunately got along better with me than I had with my own mother at their age.

By the time Harold and I married, my family was wondering whether I would ever marry, and had given up all hope of a Russian. A Yugoslav man had never been a possibility since I had never known any. And although I had spent my youth dreaming of acquiring a simple, American last name with my marriage, by its arrival date that dream had gone stale, and I loved my exotic labeling. Harold didn't see any reason to give up Hahn, but I did in the end change my name, becoming Tania rather than Tatiana on our marriage certificate.

Harold treated my parents gently and confidently. He loved their stories of exile and reconnection, their crazy parties and their singing, the three kisses everyone exchanged at Easter, the fabulous food. And he adored my mother, and eventually somehow helped the two of us learn to get along.

When my father stopped working, instead of traveling around the world as my mother always dreamed, he continued his lifelong passion of fishing. He reclaimed an old boat and with his inbred ability to repair anything that had a motor, got it in shape. He sailed from San Francisco Bay, with his brother Shura as a fishing buddy, when the salmon were running, and retained access to the Russian River for his old time favorites — the carp that I detested. Upon his retirement from his final job — having again risen to the position of engineer as he had been in Yugoslavia all those years before — his colleagues awarded him a cartoon image of himself, cigarette leaning as precariously as the small boat, hauling in a big one. Shortly after, I heard there was a picture in the *San Francisco Chronicle* of him at Fisherman's Wharf with the catch of the day — a six-foot-tall sturgeon. Since I only spoke to my father in Russian, I mistakenly translated *osetrina* to a six-foot flounder, to Harold's astonishment at the thought of this marvel.

And then, one morning at dawn, as Tolya was quietly putting on his shoes to sneak out to go fishing, Zora heard a gasp. A few hours later, at age seventy and a week after a physical examination that found him healthy, he died of a heart attack.

It was 1987, and Harold and I were trekking in the remote Himalayas of Northern India, in Kashmir and Ladakh, and didn't hear of Papa's passing until we arrived in Delhi, long after his funeral. We returned to San Francisco to find my strong Mama had become a frail old woman whose hair had started turning grey overnight. This was not the outgoing woman I had grown up with. I couldn't come to grips with this horrible transformation, with the grief that wouldn't heal.

Fortunately, I was able to move near her a short time later.

Harold and I were living at the time in Minneapolis, where we had met and married. We loved it, but knew we wouldn't stay in that cold northern climate forever. Our children—for that's how I always thought of my stepchildren Beth and Brad—were finished with high school and would both go to college in Colorado. I had just sold a technology company I had been running, and Harold suggested it was time for a lifestyle— rather than a career—decision. We decided that the San Francisco Bay Area offered everything we were looking for. It had a strong technology base for jobs, my family lived there, and we both loved it. Harold had fallen in love with it while at Stanford, and had no desire to head back to New Jersey. Besides, it had long been home for me. A few months later, we started the shift to San Francisco.

I took a job as Chief Executive of a company in Berkeley and moved to a condo in San Francisco. Harold took another year to unwind from an executive position at the large computer company in Minneapolis where we both had been working when we met, and then joined me. We spent as much time as we could with Zora, and she and I finally grew very close.

In Yugoslavia, meanwhile, Josip Broz Tito had died in 1980, and the mesh that was keeping the Yugoslav states together started fraying quickly after that. By the end of that decade, it was coming apart, first with the inevitability that was Slovenia declaring its independence, and then with the wars that started when Croatia and Bosnia, eventually followed by others, also tried to break free.

When Yugoslavia started splintering, Zora struggled with the conflict from the security of her home in San Francisco, safely distant, not comprehending what was driving the emerging viciousness of the conflict, and finally serving as the only link between sisters caught on opposing sides of the war. She couldn't do much more than call them as often as possible, send money, and worry.

One day Harold, Zora and I were sitting in her kitchen, talking as we so often did. The large bowl that always held chunks of Guittard semi-sweet baking chocolate had been offered around, and, as usual, Zora was cooking something that smelled really good. Harold teased her about her recent attempts at an exercise class at the senior center, which she quickly dropped when she realized she would have to wear shorts or tights and that men attended the class too.

"Zora, are your sisters all right?" Harold asked.

"Yes, I talk to them all the time. You know, fortunately there are no young ones in the military." Then she turned to me as she so often did and continued in Serbian. "I don't understand any of this. When we lived there the union of all the states was a strong way to keep a group of small countries from being too insignificant to matter in the world, at risk of someone attacking them or simply taking them over." I interpreted for Harold as always. We had wonderful conversations this way.

"Weren't there issues over religion?" Harold asked.

"I think this religion thing is all trumped up to give them something to fight about. The Turks were defeated many years ago; the Moslems who stayed are long integrated into the community. And no one in Yugoslavia was very religious."

"What about the issues around World War II?"

"That was awful," Zora said. She talked about the radical Croats who sided with the Nazis, and killed a lot of Serbs. And the Serbian *Partisani* who retaliated as the war was ending. "But I lived in both those countries after the war. I thought we could live in peace. I was wrong."

"Mama," I interjected, "*ti znaš*, you know, after all this time, I'm not sure I even know how you tell a Serb from a Croat. They all look the same to me; they speak almost the same language." As always, I could only speak to her in her language.

"Oh," she said, without a moment's hesitation. "It's easy. You can tell by the last name."

"By the last name?"

"Yes. If the person's last name ends in *-nič* or *-čič*, they are Croatian. If it ends in *-vič* or *-sič*, they are Serbian."

"Oh." I was amazed. "It's that simple?"

"Yes," she said, as if there could be nothing more obvious.

I turned this previously unheard of thought over in my mind for a while. I had never been able to distinguish between the various peoples in Yugoslavia. There was a myth about tall blonds on the Adriatic, or Dalmatian, coast. But really, they all just looked like white people to me. And most of them sounded alike, with more or less of the soft "e" pronunciation, what is often referred to as the *ljekavka* — strongest in central Croatia.

My mother's definition, concerning family names, was something I had never heard before, and have never been able to find any other independent substantiation of since.

"But Mama," I suddenly had a startling thought, "your name was Marinovič!"

"So?"

"Well, that ends in *–vič.*"

"Of course it does, Tania."

"But you're Istrian, and that means you are Croatian. And you told me the ending *-vič* meant Serbian."

"But remember, Tania, 400 years ago our family came from Montenegro."

"Oh, right."

She said it as if everyone knew where their families were 400 years ago. When I was young, I asked her how she knew this about her family. We had no documents of any kind that were older than our birth certificates. Even those were only translations, sneaked out of the country when we fled.

"My father talked about it all the time, Tania. How could I not know?" she answered.

I put it down to folklore, but couldn't get it out of my mind. In high school, however, I was awarded a trip from an organization called Junior Achievement to their annual conference in Indiana and added on a visit to Dyadya Zenya, who was then living with Vava in New York.

I visited the public library on Fifth Avenue and found they had a department dedicated to Slavic Studies. An elderly woman who worked there helped me research the subject of my heritage, which I described from old stories of Mama's as including Venetian ships that came to help people from Montenegro emigrate to Istria four hundred years ago.

Incredibly, the woman was able to find a variety of sources, and one did in fact talk about the Venetian Empire's need to repopulate Istria after the plagues of the Middle Ages wiped out the local populace, dropping it to 10,000 from an original 100,000 during the Roman Empire. I was shocked to learn that family myth seemed to be based in historical fact, but I lost the reference. On more recent visits, I found that the librarians had been replaced with computers, and I could not replicate my search.

But to my mother, these subjects were current and clear, requiring little explanation. She tossed out centuries-old information as if it explained everything.

"Besides," she continued, "what does it matter if we are Serbian or Croatian; we're all one people; we all speak one language. *Govorimo po našemu*. We speak our language."

"Well," I said, "right now a lot of people are killing each other over this very issue."

"Oh that," she said, as if swatting a fly rather than clarifying a debate that was tearing her family and an entire country apart. "That is just something that *prokleti* Milosevič is using to foment war. He doesn't really care about Serbs or Croats." She believed he had a power complex and wanted to keep everything under his control.

"People are unfortunately nationalistic enough that he is able to use it to generate hatred. You know, Hitler and Mussolini were able to do the same thing," Zora continued. "I've never lived in a world where someone couldn't come along and use human nature against itself."

In one brief discussion my mother clarified her perspective on a subject of confounding complexity from both a historical and sociological point of view. I suspected that this world viewpoint was what gave her the ability to live through constant turmoil, repeated exile and emigration with an amazing equanimity. There seemed nothing more to say on this subject.

I neglected to pursue, at that moment, as the country started collapsing, whether she considered herself Croatian or Serbian, or perhaps Montenegrin.

To me she was just Yugoslavian and our language Serbo-Croatian.

Together for the only time in their adult lives, the six sisters meet in Zagreb in 1973. Zora is on the right.

Tania and Harold's wedding, with the family.

CHAPTER THIRTY-TWO

Taking Zora
to Medulin

By 1992, the Yugoslavia I was born in was disappearing. Fighting had spread throughout Serbia, Croatia, and Bosnia. Zora hadn't been back to visit her sisters since long before the wars that ripped up Yugoslavia started, and she really missed them. She no longer had my father to talk to, and no one she knew in San Francisco spoke her language.

Harold and I kept offering to take her, but she deferred, worried about the fighting. We determined to pull her out of her resigned state, shake her up a bit, liven up her existence. If nothing else, we would travel in Europe together, perhaps in Italy, close to where she was born, and where she and I had lived as refugees.

"Mama, we know you've wanted to visit your country for a long time. Maybe we should go now. Harold has some vacation; I'm between jobs."

"You know it's too dangerous, Tania. They are still fighting over there." It disturbed her that it just wouldn't end, this fighting going on between countries she knew so well, countries she had lived in, countries her sisters lived in.

"Well," Harold said, "we'd like to go on a trip with you." He wanted to break through her seeming reluctance. She had been unable to bounce back from the death of my father a few years earlier. Now the continuation of this war was pulling her further down.

"Let's just go where they aren't fighting," I said. "I'd love to go to Italy, I've been studying Italian for months now. I'm ready to test it out!"

"Italy?" Mama asked.

"Yes, wouldn't you like to go to Italy?"

"Where would we go?"

"Well, I'd like to show Harold Trieste and the refugee camp we lived in when I was young. We could start by going there."

"I'd like that," interjected Harold. "But weren't you born somewhere near Trieste, Zora?"

"Sure I was. I was born in Istria, in the village of Medulin. It's the peninsula just below Trieste; it's not far from it at all."

"There's no fighting in that part of the country, is there?" asked Harold.

"Oh no, the fighting is farther south, in the border areas between Serbia and Croatia. Istria is in the far northwest. There's been no fighting there."

"Well, maybe we could start in Trieste, then explore Istria."

"But Harold," Zora said, "what about Italy? I've never been anywhere but Trieste, and you two are always going there. What's your favorite place?"

"Our favorite town is a small place just south of Genoa called Camogli. It's a little fishing village."

"Oh, goodness," her face suddenly lit up in memory. "We left for America from Genoa, on that big ship!"

"See," Harold chuckled. "You have been somewhere else in Italy."

"Well, that doesn't really count," Zora said. "We just boarded the ship there. It wasn't a real visit."

"We could start in Trieste and travel through Venice, go to Florence, and then head across to the coast," I said. "It would be fun!" I couldn't wait to try out my Italian on real Italians.

"But I think we need to go see where you were born, Zora," Harold insisted. "And Tania really wants to go back to Trieste with you. We could do all that in two weeks; it's really not that big a distance. It would be like exploring Northern California—it's no bigger!"

By then he had the atlas out, and was drawing lines. "Let's see. Trieste is just a few miles east of Venice, on the Adriatic, and right on the border. Immediately across the border to the south is the Istrian peninsula. It looks like the city of Pula, at the southern tip of Istria, is less than a hundred miles south of Trieste. I bet we could even take a boat there!"

"I hadn't thought of it that way," I admitted. "Makes you wonder why we have waited this long."

Harold and I looked at each other, then at Mama. I was waiting for her to tell us it was impossible.

And then Zora uttered the unexpected words that actually set us off on this adventure: *"Ti znaš, Tania, ne možemo više čekati.* You know, Tania, we can't wait forever for this war to end."

CHAPTER THIRTY-THREE

Finding
Cousin Milan

Who was that vibrant woman? I wondered a few weeks later, far from that kitchen in San Francisco. *Did I know her?*

She looked a bit like my mother: tiny, short dark hair complementing a black-eyed sparkle, linen dress showing a bit of knee, slender legs, and with a figure still close enough to nubile for a woman way beyond that stage of life. Her feet were shod in comfortable walking shoes that nevertheless had a bit of heel to accentuate an ankle beautiful enough to justify the painful bunions caused by years of artfully heeled feet.

But wait! This woman's face pointed upwards — not submissively — grandly, as though bestowing a gift on the person she addressed. She wore a big smile and carried herself with a flirtatious bearing. My mother's eyes didn't sparkle. They hadn't since Tolya had died. And I hardly remembered that freely bestowed smile — let alone one given to a stranger.

Who was that woman, and why was she standing in a foreign town, flirting with a tall, handsome, white-haired gentleman?

Those thoughts ran through my mind as we travelled to the small town of Medulin, Istria, to look for Zora's birthplace and her maternal Uncle, Bogdan.

We landed in Trieste, Italy and a few days later took a taxi to Pula, the city on the southern tip of Istria, which was quite close to Medulin. The taxi was our only alternative as rental companies, because of the war, would not let us rent a car in Italy and enter the former Yugoslavia with it. No buses or trains plied that route, and boats went only between Venice and Istria, not Trieste and Istria.

It started in the taxicab. Harold had no sooner seated Zora in the front seat than she recognized from the driver's accent that they shared a common language; one which was certainly not Italian. She learned he had fled from Serbia, and they talked non-stop *po našemu* for the hour it took to arrive.

In Pula, we checked into a deserted and slightly worn hotel on the water and then stepped out to find the car rental office. When we became briefly disoriented, it was Zora, and not I, who stopped the stranger walking toward us and asked questions. I just stood and watched, entranced. It was the first time I had an opportunity to observe my mother in the land of her birth. She opened like a flower that spreads its petals when warmed by the sun.

A few hours later Zora, Harold and I ended up, in that late summer of 1992, in Medulin, lost, wandering through the streets of the small, deserted town. We were on a mission to find an uncle Zora had seen once in her life, fifty years earlier on a visit with her own mother shortly after the end of World War II. We had searched both for the house my mother was born in and for her uncle Bogdan Rojnič. Her only relative, he had stayed in Istria after the Italians took over and forced Mama's family out. But Bogdan was simply not to be found. We had just learned that our last possible source, an older postman, had left town for the weekend. It seemed hopeless, and the depressive atmosphere of a country beset by wars didn't help.

Harold tried to get Mama to talk about the past, about her village. The stories bore no resemblance to the slowly crumbling town around us. It was fun listening, and we sat in the café for a while, sipping coffee and eating *torte* that reminded Harold of the ones Mama would bake for him at home. But we didn't make progress on coming up with new places to search.

Despondent, we decided to head back toward Pula. In three days' time we were taking one of the last boats of the season from Rovinj, just up the coast, to Venice. Maybe we could re-invigorate ourselves after lunch to go explore the area more deeply than we had done so far. There had to be some landmark, some memory we could help Zora trigger.

As we pulled out of the center of town, we passed a small bank on the side of the road. I pulled over, not realizing how significant that simple act would be.

"We should get some local money." I was used to being the organizer. But when I got out of the car, Zora followed.

"I want to have some money also," she announced. A new Zora was continuing to evolve, a woman confident in her surroundings, and in command of her world. I had grown up with a mother who was confident in her own home, and sure of her role as my mother, but not completely at ease in the larger world where everyone spoke English, her fourth and probably weakest language.

"I could get some for all of us." I said.

"*Hvala*, thanks, Tania. I will get my own."

Two young women sat behind the counter, deep in conversation. The unexpectedness of strangers was clear from the expression on their faces as they glanced up.

"*Gospodje*," one of them said. It meant "Ladies," and the intonation, with a slight questioning lift at the end, indicated *hello, welcome, how are you? who are you? what do you want?* and *do you understand me?* all in that one word. We instantly understood its implicit complexity.

Zora approached the one on the left saying, "*Dobar dan. Kako ste?* Good day. How are you?"

"Good day. Very well, thank you. How can I help you?"

"Can you change dollars?" Mama asked.

"If you have a valid passport, we can."

I turned to the other young woman. We discussed exchange rates and whether they accepted traveler's checks. I heard a lively conversation going on next to us, but wasn't really paying too much attention. I assumed it was polite small talk, as one might have while converting dollars.

Until, that is, the woman working with me suddenly jolted upright and said: "But that's my grandfather!"

"What?" asked the other one.

"That's my grandfather."

"Who's your grandfather?"

"The man she is looking for is my grandfather."

"Your grandfather Daro?" asked the young woman working with my mother, totally confused. Zora now turned wide-eyed to the one in front of me. "The one who died a few years ago?"

"Yes, my grandfather Daro is, or was, the Bogdan she is looking for."

Zora had apparently been telling the story of our fruitless search for her uncle. The young woman she was talking to continued, perplexed. "But your grandfather was not called Bogdan, like this woman's uncle. Your grandfather was Daro."

The young woman, who told us her name was Tamara, said, "Well, he was also Bogdan Rojnič. After the first war, when the Italians were here, he officially changed his name to Dario—Daro for short. They had to if they wanted to stay and keep their jobs and homes. Slavic names were outlawed. So at work he was Daro, but at home he stayed Bogdan. Is that who you are looking for?"

"*Bože moj.* Oh my God," said Zora. "Now I remember hearing he changed his name when we visited, but I forgot all about that. No wonder we couldn't find him!"

"You mean you've been here before?" the young woman named Tamara asked.

"Yes, my mother and I came just after the Second World War," answered Zora. "We saw Bogdan and Roža and their son Matte."

"*Bože moj*! Matte is my father. But he is called Milan. He still lives in the family home."

"Oh dear. I can hardly believe this," said Zora. "But actually, except for your blond hair, I can see the family resemblance."

"But I had blond hair, Mama," I interjected, laughing.

"Well, mine has some help," said Tamara. "But I don't think I heard about that visit. It was long before I was born. How, exactly, are you related to Bogdan?"

"I'm his niece, Zora. My mother was Katarina Rojnič, my father was Martin Marinovič."

"*Bože moj*," said an amazed Tamara one more time. "I've heard so much about your family. You lived across the road, didn't you? And didn't you have lots of sisters? And one of you went to America?"

"Yes, there were seven of us children, all girls. I was the last one born here, the next two came after our parents fled."

"What year were you born in?" Tamara asked.

"I was born in 1922."

"And you've been gone ever since!"

"Yes, yes. My parents left Istria then. I grew up in Serbia and Croatia, and I've been living in America a long time. Since a few years after my visit here after the war. Your father was an idealistic young man then, and the Italians hadn't even left yet."

"Well, things have changed a lot since then. Hardly anyone even understands Italian any more. We also seem to be living through another war." Tamara shook her head and paused. Then she continued. "And, as you just heard, Bogdan died some years ago."

"Oh," said Zora. "I was afraid that might be the case. He would have been very old by now."

"Yes, that's true. Even Milan is already a grandfather. My son Marko is ten."

"My goodness, all these years . . ." continued Zora. "But that's wonderful about your son!"

"And you said your name is Zora?" I could see a deeper question in her eyes, but I didn't understand it.

Zora knew her name meant Dawn in Croatian, and that her parents had given it to her in a futile hope for a new dawn in their country after World War I. It was not an uncommon name where she grew up. But, as we were soon to learn, people of my mother's generation didn't have Croatian names, not in Istria.

"Yes, yes, I'm Zora," Mama replied quickly, "and this is my daughter Tania."

"*Jako prijatno*! Very nice to meet you!" The young woman turned to me. "So you're from America then. Which part?"

"We live in San Francisco."

"*I vi govorite po našemu*! And you speak our language!" she exclaimed.

"Of course," my mother immediately interjected, proudly. "Both my children *govore po našemu*. I promised my mother they would, and there was no way I would disappoint her."

"Was your husband a Serb?" the young woman asked. I wondered briefly why she didn't say "a Croatian," but the thought slipped my mind almost before I was aware of it.

"No, he was Russian. They spoke Russian with him."

"*Joj, joj, joj*. You lived in America all this time, and your children spoke both your languages. And we think it's too much to ask that our children learn English, which the whole world is now using. And they can listen to it on TV!"

"Do you speak English?" I asked.

"I'm afraid not. But it doesn't matter, you speak *po našemu* perfectly! Wait until I tell my father you are here! He will be so pleased." She clapped her hands in front of her in glee. "Will you have time to visit my family?"

"We would love to visit your family!" I replied. "It's the main reason we came here, along with seeing the home my mother was born in."

"I will call them and tell them you are here. Can you come back in a couple of hours when I am off work and they have had time to get ready?"

"Of course," I replied. "My husband is in the car; we were just on our way back to our hotel in Pula. We can come later this afternoon, but we don't know where to go!"

"Of course," she laughed. "I'll meet you at the town square and lead you up, all right? It's very simple, we're just halfway up the hill on the street from the sea to the church."

"We know, we know," I muttered ruefully, almost to myself. We had followed that description endlessly while looking for a house that was simply not to be found.

"That would be lovely," said Zora. "We can be back by four, can't we, Tania?"

"Definitely," I said. "We'll see you then!"

CHAPTER THIRTY-FOUR

Visitors
from America

Matte, or Milan as everyone called him, was
beside himself with joy.

"*Došli ste iz Amerike da nas vidite*! You came from
America to see us!" he cried as we walked in. Everyone hugged and kissed, and exclaimed at the surprise of our visit, overwhelmed at the random
chance that brought us to Tamara's counter at the
bank.

Milan learned that Zora had lost her husband,
and they exchanged children's stories and spent a lot
of time just sitting quietly and peacefully, absorbing.
Amazingly, Milan's birthday was that week and we
were invited to the party on the following night.

At the celebration, tears and conversation flowed as
if from a fire hose. Fifty years worth of stories as the

older generation caught up on family and experiences. Those our age wanted to learn about life in America, and hear our thoughts about what was happening in Yugoslavia — or the country once known by that name.

The youngest ones had never met anyone from America. Tamara's ten-year-old son Marko wouldn't leave my 6'6" tall husband's side.

"NBA, NBA," he chanted at first. There was a famous and famously wealthy Croatian basketball player in America — Dražen Petrović, perhaps one of the best shooters ever — and all the young boys dreamed of the game as a way of escaping the drama and bad luck that was plaguing their own country.

Marko also ran around shouting "Rat, tat, tat! Rat, tat," and pointing an imaginary machine gun. "Eliot Ness, Eliot Ness!" he shouted the name of the legendary prohibition agent from the 1920s.

I was afraid Harold would get sick laughing over this. Were those the impressions of America held by a ten-year-old in a war-torn country on the edge of Europe, in late 1992? Basketball players and prohibition agents?

It immediately transported me back to San Francisco in 1954. My brother and I, newly arrived, couldn't speak a word of English. We needed to learn, and fast. But before we did, we would tear around the house with broken paint-stirring sticks in our hands, our version of toy guns. Periodically one of us would face the other and snarl nonsense out of the side of our mouths, Al Capone style. I supposed Eliot Ness in 1992 Istria was only marginally odder than two young immigrants playing Al Capone when pretending to be Americans forty years earlier.

The birthday party for Milan included the entire extended family that was still in Istria. Several cousins had gone off to work in Germany. Those who — like my mother's family — left when the Italians took over had never come back, even after the Italians were kicked out in 1947.

While Harold and I talked to the young people, Zora caught up on the family history. I heard vague references to someone in Argentina, something more about the relatives in *Deda Marinović's* house. There was clearly ongoing tension, but I was too busy translating for Harold and didn't pay much attention. I was just thrilled she was absorbed in her family's embrace.

We ate all my favorite childhood foods: grilled lamb skewers called *ražnići*, ground meat formed into small sausage shaped rolls called *čevapčići*, grilled Hungarian peppers, and fresh tomato, cucumber and feta salad. It all could have come from my mother's kitchen, but it tasted much better in the land where she was born.

"Tell us about the rest of your family, Zora. We haven't heard from anyone since the war started. They used to come here occasionally, in the summer," said Milan. "Have you been able to stay in touch with them?"

"I have," Zora said, "but it has been very hard."

Zora's sisters' families were now a group comprised of Serbs, Croats, Macedonians and Bosnians, and their religions included Catholic, Orthodox and Moslem. During the war, they were split into opposing camps and had no ability to communicate with each other.

Zora was the connector between the sisters. She could reach each of them by telephone, even though they couldn't reach each other. At first, they were all anxious to hear about each other. Then it started. First the husbands started cursing the Serbs, or the Croats, depending on who it was. Soon it became clear that family was not necessarily exempt from the offenses committed by both sides and that neither side was anxious to forgive or forget. Then the younger generation, those my age, became more nationalistic than their parents. After all, these were not their brothers or sisters, but cousins whom they rarely saw and could easily move into the camp of the "other side." Eventually, Mama just talked to each sister about her life and her family. It felt like the only safe territory left. They stopped discussing the other sisters, or the war, or politics.

Zora told them about all this, but also told them how happy she was that each of the sisters still had her family to take care of her.

"Slavića said it best, you know," Zora continued. "She is surrounded by her six children and all the grandchildren. She doesn't care what country she lives in, she just wants to give them all the love in her heart and to make sure they all grow up knowing they are loved. Maybe then they can someday all love each other again: Croats, Serbs, Macedonians, Bosnians."

"Maybe," said Milan, but you could tell he very much doubted it.

Tania and Zora visiting Medulin in the 1990s. Harold was taking
the picture, Milan (also called Matte) is sitting, and young Marco
is to the left.

CHAPTER THIRTY-FIVE

Zora learns her real name

We found our way easily back to the house the next day. Zora was specifically not invited to go into the house across the street, the one she had been born in and which had been sold at a bargain to relatives. The two families still never spoke, and we didn't go into the reasons for this animosity.

After the requisite cup of Turkish coffee, we walked up the hill to the church and cemetery. Like so much of the area, it was rundown and looked almost abandoned. We searched in vain for old tombstones. My ideas of documenting the family tree vanished as we walked around, talking.

"Oh, you won't find any old tombstones here," Milan said. "First of all, the old ones with Slavic names were all torn down by the Italian dictatorship

in the early twenties. And we reuse gravesites here."
He told us that every fifty years or so they take out
the old bones and bury the newly deceased in the
same spot again. "Otherwise this cemetery wouldn't
hold everyone. You know this area has been occupied since before Roman times. This graveyard is
ancient."

Mama started talking about her last visit. "The
last time I was here," Zora said, "I was told that the
authorities destroyed Slavic records. I never did see
my birth certificate."

"I don't think your paperwork would have been
affected," Milan said. "Weren't you born in 1922?"

"Yes, in July."

"Well, the Italians had been ceded Istria by then.
Those records were probably kept because there
were no Slavic names recorded from the early 1920s
on. That's why my name is Milan."

"How can that be? My name is Zora, and I'm sure
it was recorded at the church. My father said he met
with Father Carlo personally."

"He might have kept it to himself, to avoid upset-
ting your mother," said Milan.

"Kept what to himself?" Zora asked.

But Milan had moved on. "I think you were born
just before the crisis that forced your family to leave,
right?"

"Yes. I was born in 1922, and Mussolini became the Italian Prime Minister a few months later."

"Well, we can check at the church. They might have something. I doubt that you are part of the Italian Civil records. They only recorded the people who stayed. Do you want to go ask?"

"That would be amazing," Harold said. He didn't know the town his grandparents came from, and here we were, with a possible direct connection to Zora's birth.

Fortunately it was Sunday, and we were able to talk to the young pastor, Father Dragan. His records were far from complete, but he did remember some old books from long before his time.

"The old pastors hid away some of the books or made copies, if possible. Let me see what I can find. There weren't many from that period. It was when they were transitioning to government records rather than just church ones."

"Marinovič, Marinovič. Here's one from January 1919, shortly after the end of the first war. Born to Martin Marinovič and Katarina Rojnič. Girl, name of Slava."

"Oh my, that's my sister Slavića. Mine would be three years later, on July 21." Zora seemed to want to move past that information quickly.

"Let me see if the next book is here." He kept searching.

We waited expectantly.

"Here it is," he said. "Yes, here it is. July 21, 1922. Born to Martin Marinovič and Katarina Rojnič."

"Oh, Mama," I said, excited. "That has to be you." It was like being in the middle of an adventure story.

"Here you are," said the pastor. "It says: 'Girl, name of *Albina*.'"

"That's not me!" exclaimed Zora. "Let me see that."

He passed the book to her, looking concerned.

"The date is right, and my parents' names are correct. But who is *Albina*? I've never heard of an *Albina*."

"I'm afraid that's you, Zora," Milan said.

"What do you mean, me?"

"Well, think about it. *Albina* is Italian for Zora, or dawn."

"Oh," Zora whispered. "Oh."

She just kept staring at the page with those words handwritten in ink on paper that was starting to yellow.

"I told you," said Milan, "that they didn't allow Slavic names in those days. Your father must have chosen the closest name he could. I know I was given the name Milan because Matte, their original choice, wasn't allowed."

Mama just looked at him, then at me, without saying a word. She backed away from us and sat down, speechless. She had just learned, at age seventy, that her father had kept something this important secret from them all those years. He was long buried, even if not in this cemetery.

What else might we not know about her family?

"*Albina*," she said. "*Albina*." She paused for a moment, remembering how much her parents had hated Mussolini and the Italians.

"*Albina*. You never knew that was the name they gave you?" said Harold, breaking into her thoughts. His next words caught all of us by surprise. "What a beautiful name!"

She stared at him, and slowly a big smile grew on her face. "*Albina*. It is beautiful. Thank you, Harold."

"Shall we call you that from now on?" He smiled down at her, and she relaxed and hit his arm as she did when they teased.

"Oh no," she said. "I think you can stay with Zora. *Albina* might be a nice name, but it really doesn't have anything to do with me."

"Doesn't it make you angry?" Milan asked, clearly not expecting this reaction.

"No, I don't think it does. My father probably didn't have any choice. And you know, I didn't live here through those times when the Italians were here. I don't dislike them. The Italians in Trieste took us in when we had to flee Yugoslavia. They were good to us."

"But what about the home you lost because of them, here?"

"For my parents that was important. They were never to have a house of their own again. But I never lived there. I never thought about it. It doesn't feel like my home."

"What does feel like home, Zora?" Milan continued.

Zora looked at me; she looked at Harold. I saw the new Zora, the reinvigorated proud woman who walked tall here, as she hadn't since my father died. I didn't know what she would say.

"My home is in San Francisco." She nodded her head and smiled as she caught my eye, as if taking in her own words. "I have loved it from the day we moved in. I am an American. My children are Americans. I can't imagine living anywhere else. And I certainly don't want to hate anyone for things that happened years ago."

"But don't you miss our country, your country?"

"In the beginning, I missed my family terribly. Especially when we lived in the Campo. But I've been in America almost forty years, my children grew up there. They are very successful. It is my home."

I could tell that just saying that was confirming its truth for Zora. To Harold and me, it seemed that Zora blossomed in this place where everyone spoke her language. But in spite of her comfort in this environment, being here reaffirmed the depth of her love for her home in San Francisco.

"I can't imagine leaving here," Milan said, sweeping his hand over the town, over the sea. "It's part of who I am. I will be buried here."

"You know, Milan," Zora said, "sometimes the choices that are forced on us end up being the right ones after all. I am so happy not to be living through one more war. It is remote and incomprehensible. And my children thank me all the time for where they live. They are truly Americans."

"And I am an American," she finished the discussion firmly, and with a clear pride.

"But they speak our language!"

"We do, Milan," I said. "But everyone in America comes from somewhere. We like to remember where we came from, but we don't want to go back.'

"I understand," he said. "But I often wonder what that is like, to leave everything behind. It feels terrifying. I was still young when you left, Zora, but even then I had nightmares about someone else moving into our house. I promised myself that my children would live in this house no matter what it took!"

"And my mother gave up her home but made me promise my children would speak her language." Zora said. "I agreed long before I knew I would marry a Russian, or that he would be persecuted in his adopted land, or that my children would leave their country as infants. But I have lived up to my promise, as you have lived up to yours. The future is in their hands now."

"But wouldn't you like to live here?" Milan asked Harold. Clearly in his eyes there was no place more beautiful than his little village on the Adriatic coast.

"I love being able to visit such a beautiful place, and to meet wonderful people like you," Harold replied, tactful as ever. "And I'd love to come back and play basketball with your grandsons!"

As I continued translating for Harold during the entire visit, I blessed his ability to make everyone feel that their opinion was valid while retaining his in a way that didn't offend. We had figured out, by then, that their impressions of America were not necessarily very positive. Eliot Ness and gangs, racial tensions and dire poverty in inner cities populated their version of our country, interspersed with pop music and Hollywood interpretations of life. And here, where we saw senseless wars, they saw a battle for freedom and equality.

We all saw a beautiful landscape, and we all understood that a unique way of life had been sacrificed all those years ago. But we now lived on disconnected shores, separated by a history that could not be restarted like a Hollywood movie. Perhaps the strongest thing our common genes had provided was the positive outlook on life that made each of us believe we had the preferred life.

As we walked back to the house, I reflected on what I had just learned. A language and a country of birth created a unique link between Mama and me, a uniquely powerful gift. But home would always be something we carried inside us. It would always be with us.

No one could take our home away.

CHAPTER THIRTY-SIX

San Sabba secrets

Our discoveries on that trip were not limited to Istria or to Zora's early life. On our last night in Istria, Zora, Harold and I went to dinner at a small restaurant near the hotel. We sat on a beautiful patio, grapevines covering the arbor, a lone musician keeping us company. Tourists had been frightened away by the wars and the locals couldn't afford to eat out. The platter of fresh shellfish we were served was among the best we had ever eaten. The rest of the Mediterranean was getting fished out, but the crises here had created a unique culinary opportunity that we savored.

We talked about all we had seen, heard, and learned on our visit.

"How wonderful that we found your Cousin Milan, Zora, and were able to celebrate his birthday with him! It's an evening I won't soon forget," Harold said.

"And I am so glad I got to see the house I was born in and visit the cemetery," said my mother.

"It is all quite incredible," I said. "We've been gone less than a week and so many things are not what we thought they were just a few days ago. Starting in Trieste and then continuing here."

"I know," Zora said. "Harold, remember you asked me if I knew my uncle's name and I laughed at you?"

"Yes," Harold said. "I felt incredibly silly at the time."

"And now I learned that not only did I not know his name, I didn't even know mine!" She turned to me and continued in Serbian, "*Bože moj*! Dear God. I thought I was coming home, but instead I feel like I entered a different world."

"Mama, do you really not mind finding that your name was recorded as *Albina*?"

"I don't care about that, but I am sorry I didn't understand how much it all must have disturbed my father."

"And speaking of learning things weren't all they seemed, the things we heard and saw in Trieste were pretty shocking as well," I said.

"Oh yes, we haven't had much time to talk about that, but I am still stunned," Zora said.

While Zora, Harold and I were in Trieste, we wanted to visit Campo San Sabba, the refugee camp my family had lived in for four years, from 1950 to 1954. I was almost five years old when we left, and had very vivid memories of it. I think part of the reason for that was just the vast change in our lives after we left the camp. If you lived in one town or one house for a long time, I suspect it would be hard to remember details of the timeline of your early life. But for me, everything changed. There was the drama of departure, of leaving a place my parents couldn't get away from fast enough, but which to me was filled with people I loved and whom I had no wish to leave. Then there was a new country, a new language, new friends, a whole new world.

Campo, or *logor* and *lager* in Serbian and Russian, was kept alive through conversation. In San Francisco, we lived in a house that was peopled with friends and relatives from the camp.

When I was in college, I took a summer to travel in Europe. Of course I went to Trieste. I was traveling very cheaply, and stayed at the youth hostel next to the Miramare Castle, on the coast just west of the city, toward Venice.

I made my way to the center of the city, and immediately recognized the old Savoia Palace Hotel, right on the harbor, where the sea meets the city.

Then I had to find the camp—*Campo*. But I wasn't worried, I knew the name, after all. I hadn't thought about the simple fact that the word *Campo* just means camp in Italian, and that I actually had no useful identifying information. None.

I just followed my mental image of where it would be, heading past the stadium, toward the port. I found it in a rundown industrial neighborhood.

In that summer of 1968, the entire camp was still there, and was still recognizable. The large red brick factory building that my aunts and uncles had lived in, across the street from the barracks where we resided, was boarded up and abandoned, in a state of serious disrepair. The wooden barracks were also still there, although severely run down, with warped siding, missing doors, and garbage strewn all over. I was reluctant to approach the people who were hanging around; it somehow felt private. I didn't feel comfortable intruding—something I have had time to regret.

I was later told it was populated by *gypsies*—a throwaway name for the dispossessed and homeless in that part of the world. It was an encampment the city wanted to eliminate. It all looked much as it had in my mind, and I was too young to feel the deep curiosity and nostalgia that another twenty years would develop.

Our visit to Trieste in 1992 was very different. I was no longer a college student traveling on the cheap. I was a successful executive bringing her mother back to a place she had left as a homeless refugee, dependent on others for her very survival.

"Harold, I think we should book the Palace Hotel in Trieste for our visit," I said as I explored the Internet on my laptop computer.

"The Palace? What's it like?"

"Well, it's not the most expensive place in town, but it's pretty close. It's certainly the most ostentatious. It's right in the center of town, on the water. I remember it from when I was a kid."

"Tania, do you really remember it? You were pretty young when you left."

"Well, I'm not really sure. I'd like to think I do. But it looks like an old Austro-Hungarian palace for wealthy travelers. I have this incredible desire to make sure Mama goes back in style. She left on borrowed money, and they traveled in third class or worse. I want her to go back in first."

"Will she be comfortable in such a fancy place?"

"I don't know, but I think so."

"I'm not so sure," he said. I knew Harold was thinking of his own mother, secure in New Jersey near her place of birth, uncomfortable unless she was in familiar territory.

But Zora was different. For someone who showed up in America with nothing, she had an innate sense of style about her. She was always perfectly groomed, while I, her daughter, was a true child of the 1960s who dressed properly only when it was required for business. In her seventies, Zora still wore heels because they looked sophisticated. She lived off a modest pension from my father, but didn't spend it all, still in the habit of saving money every year, *na svaki slučaj*, just in case. She had learned never to trust life to provide a predictable future, and she was taking no chances.

My childhood vacations with my parents had been spent in converted chicken coops on the Stanislaus River and later in tents on a mountain lake in the Sierras. After my father retired, they had taken a few longer trips. But since he died, Zora never went anywhere, which was why we wanted to make sure this trip worked.

"Well, first class is fine with me!" Harold said, grinning. He had always teased me about my fiscal prudence.

"Now that we can finally afford it, I'm getting her the best room. I'm going to call and see if the one with a balcony overlooking the sea is available. It's really not that expensive, anyway. September's a bit off-season."

I booked the room, organized a few more hotels and cars, and a few weeks later we flew to Italy.

The taxi from the Trieste airport dropped us off at the front entry of the Savoia Excelsior Palace Hotel. A uniformed doorman came out to get our bags. Zora, seemingly immune to jet lag, bounced out of the car and swept up the stairs as if this were her normal practice; as if she were used to fancy doormen and quiet grand spaces, to people anticipating her every need, as if she had never been bothered to open her own door.

I walked up to the front desk, ready to use the Italian I had been studying for the trip.

"I have two rooms for you. I see you specifically requested the balcony room, the best room in the house," said the front desk clerk in perfect English. "I assume that is for you and your husband?"

"No, actually, that one is for my mother," I explained.

The elegantly dressed clerk looked at Zora, perhaps recognizing a kindred spirit. She nodded her head, and a large smile broke out on his face. You could tell he decided right then that she must be the one paying the bill. "May I have your passport, please, Madame, and we'll show you immediately to your room."

Zora graciously allowed him to fawn over her and was swept away from us toward the elevator, not troubled at all about staying first class on her return trip to Trieste.

We explored Trieste, but our most important goal was visiting *campo*. This time we had come armed with the name: Campo San Sabba. We asked the concierge for directions.

"Ah, you want to see the memorial at the Risiera di San Sabba."

"What memorial?" I asked, wondering if I had misunderstood.

"Well, the Risiera has been made into a memorial to the people who suffered there during the war. But were you there during the war?"

"No, we lived there after the war."

"After the war?"

"Yes," I said. "We lived there from 1950 to 1954."

"I believe the Risiera was closed at the end of the war," he said.

"What is a risiera?" I asked.

"A rice factory. It was an old rice factory."

"That's right," said Zora. "I remember. The big brick building was a rice factory, I knew that!"

We ended the confusing conversation and made our way in the direction of the Stadium and down the hill to the camp. The barracks were gone; a large warehouse for the grocery store COOP had been built in their place. But most amazingly, the old rice factory building had a newly built brick entryway.

We walked through the new passage into a building Zora and I had known intimately. She and I made our way to the open courtyard, and stood staring at the walls that surrounded us. We both instinctively faced the direction that led to the rooms my aunts and uncles had lived in, up an internal staircase to the second floor. But the upper floors had crumbled and were shut off. There was no way to enter them.

We learned that the camp's previous use was as a concentration camp during World War II. The only one in Italy with crematoria, it had been occupied by Jews, Serbian partisans, and others considered undesirable by the Nazis and Fascists.

Horrific things had happened in this place, and our family had spent years living with the spirits of that horror. Zora and I were both crying by the time this sank in. As hard as the memory of that time might have been for her, it paled in contrast to what those people had experienced. We felt shell-shocked. Instead of retrieving memories tempered by the passage of time, we were encountering new horrors: unexpected, unwelcome, and almost impossible to absorb.

We also learned that the Displaced Persons camp set up in this place after the war had sheltered two primary groups of people. The one we had been part of were those, mostly Russians, who were displaced by the post-war spread of Communism.

The others were Italians displaced when Istria was given back to Yugoslavia.

A few years earlier I had bought my brother an old copy of *LIFE magazine* from the week of September 11, 1947—his birthday. Incredibly, the cover story was about the return of Istria to Yugoslavia from Italy that very week. It turned out that the land taken from my mother's family at her birth was returned to her country at the birth of her son.

Just as my family had been persecuted twenty-five years earlier by Italians, the Italians were then persecuted by the Yugoslavs. Many lost their homes and fled the country. The issue was still so raw at the end of 2013, as I was researching this story, that Wikipedia temporarily froze their articles on the subject because of contention and disagreement.

That same peace treaty of 1947 established the Free Territory of Trieste under the protection of the United Nations. Its official languages were Slovene, Italian and Croatian, and the government was administered by American and British forces. Those were the politics that made it possible for our family to flee to Trieste a short time later. Those were the politics that settled my family in the same refugee camp with the Italians who now had to wait for homes in Italy.

Our conversation over that memorable shellfish dinner was wide-ranging and lasted long into the evening. We finished our trip in Istria the next day, and headed on a ferry to Venice and the rest of our voyage. The war that was tearing up Yugoslavia kept us from heading deeper into the country to visit Mama's sisters, but had inadvertently created the opening that allowed us to visit the place of her birth instead. Thus we had visited the home Mama was born in, met her relatives, learned about Daro and *Albina*. We finished our dinner in a place that was deserted and just waiting for another war to end — a place that might once have been familiar and dear to my mother was now someone else's troubled homeland.

For me, visiting her homeland with my mother opened a door to the countries of her birth and mine. It started a search that was to continue for many years, and added a depth to my life that I could not have imagined as I set up the travel plans for five short days in Istria.

It also brought me a new mother — a woman who was different from the exile, the foreigner with a heavy accent who had raised me in America. A woman confident of belonging, and one who consciously owned her home. A woman who now knew she was no longer a refugee, but a woman choosing to live in a land that had given her, and all of us, refuge.

A woman who shared her heritage and her language with me. A woman who taught me my mother tongue, taught me to speak *po našemu*.

Mama blossomed there in a way we hadn't experienced since the death of my father. She was in her element, leading the way, talking, laughing, almost flirting. As she told Harold, this was not a foreign country, this was her country.

The words that will stay with me from that trip, however, were the ones Zora said to Milan: "My home is with my family, in America."

We had an incredible journey to her country. A journey that taught us that her homeland was deeply important and precious, but it was no longer home.

Tania and Sasha with their cousins in Novi Sad, Serbia.

Tania and Sasha with cousins in Medulin.

Sasha with Zagreb cousins.

Epilogue

Some years after Mama's death, when Yugoslavia was little more that a memory, my brother Sasha and I returned to explore and learn more about our past. We wanted to visit Medulin, the place where Mama was born, and also to see our cousins in Zagreb and Belgrade and Novi Sad. We organized parties to bring them together, only to realize that we, the *Amerikanci*, were the only ones maintaining the links to the past. For the two of us, who grew up with stories about this extended group of cousins, our lives felt tightly linked. We knew how much my mother regretted having to leave her sisters behind and how tied she felt to all of them. From America, Yugoslavia looked like a small country. We just assumed they had all stayed close.

But for them, life moved on. They had far bigger issues than staying in touch with relatives in Serbia or

Croatia. Other than the sale of some land in Medulin, there was no reason to communicate. Half the cousins, after all, now lived in countries that had fought vicious battles against each other—devastating wars that had impacted all of them. They were not raising their children to have deep connections to the families of their grandparents. All of Zora's generation were gone, and our own were getting into their sixties and seventies.

Zora had lost everything she owned twice in her life. As an infant, her parents fled Istria and left behind all their material possessions. All they brought with them was a large family and a common language. Zora promised her own mother she would pass that legacy of love and language on to her children.

Little could she imagine, as Katarina lay dying, how challenging this might be. Zora married a man who was Russian, and who had his own beloved language to pass on. And then she was forced to flee her country with little more than her clothes one more time. But she held to her promise, passing on her love of family and language—speaking *po našemu*, in our way, with her children. She did so even though she was the only person in our lives who spoke that language.

Because we could speak *po našemu*, in our travels Sasha and I learned a lot about life in those countries and many new stories about our family. And we learned that our grandparents' respective families — Rojnić and Marinović ancestors — were involved in a feud over houses and land in Medulin.

"I suppose we might have expected something like this," said Sasha. "This is the Balkans, after all. Why should our family be any different?"

I again looked up the word "Balkanize" in the dictionary and was reminded that it means the break up of a group into smaller and often hostile units.

There was one moment in history when things were different. Most people know little about this land, but unfortunately even those who have given the area more than a passing thought often believe that Yugoslavia, like many countries of the Middle East, was cobbled together by the Allied Powers in the aftermath of World War I. But I had heard about its creation from my mother and had studied the subject at university.

All the countries, and Croatia in particular, were vitally interested in the union in 1918.

Croatia, under Austro-Hungary, until that empire crumbled with their loss in World War I, was then threatened with falling under the domination of Italy. Slovenia was in a similar situation, and only Serbia had its own independent government, which became the foundation of the new Kingdom. The

Southern Slav union, Yugoslavia, was their creation, and it was devastating to the Slavic people of Istria—and my mother's family in particular—when their home was instead given to the Italians. Zora's parents fled to the safety of the union of Slavs, hoping to raise a family under its protection.

That safety was unfortunately transitory. Yugoslavia fell apart in World War II, pulled itself back together for about forty years under the Communist government of Josip Broz Tito, and then tore itself up in the Yugoslav wars at the end of the twentieth century. My grandparents and their descendants repeatedly lost everything because of the endless conflicts that just wouldn't let go of their homelands.

Sasha and I started life poor in possessions, but, in the end, we gained everything. We were fortunate both in our parents' character and in their decision to wait for acceptance by America. Growing up in this country, the land our parents paid such a price to reach, allowed us, like many Americans, to be both fully integrated and yet able to hold onto our roots and our parents' languages. It is a unique gift, but one that is acknowledged and accepted in this country of ours. Without question we are Americans in every sense of the word, and comfortable in that skin.

In fleeing her country for the final time as an adult in 1950, Zora left behind not just family and possessions. She left behind her native land's conflicts. She taught us love for all of its people. We feel tied to a larger family in the Balkans and have the joy of connecting to people and stories that enrich our lives because of who Zora was, because she refused to let conflict dominate and ruin our lives.

It was in 1992, while visiting her place of birth after almost fifty years in America, that I watched my mother both blossom in her original culture and acknowledge her deep adoption of her new homeland. It was going back to her first *home* that let her recognize where *home* really was. It was where she lived, where she raised her children, where she would stay until she died. It is that sense of *home* that she passed on to us, a place that had nothing to do with land that was fought over or old battles. It was a place where she would feed and nurture us. A place where we always knew we were loved, and where we would build our own families in the framework of that love.

Mama developed dementia and eventually forgot English and Russian. She would chatter away in Serbian to anyone who would listen, understanding them and assuming they could understand her. In the end, it was only Sasha and I who could speak with her.

So for a final time, just before she died, my mother once again lost everything but her language — everything that mattered. When material possessions became irrelevant, as they inevitably do, it meant more than we could have ever imagined. This time it was her own mind that robbed her, but fortunately she chose the precious legacy of voice to pass on to me. It lets me tell her, wherever she is, *po našemu*, that I love her. Always.

Ljubim te, Mama. Uvek.

About the Author

Tania Romanov Amochaev was born in Belgrade, Serbia of two displaced émigrés—a White Russian father and a Croatian mother—and spent her childhood in San Sabba, a refugee camp in Trieste. After arriving in America on the *SS Constitution*, Tania attended San Francisco's public schools. She earned a degree in mathematics from the University of California at Berkeley in 1970, graduating while the school was on strike in protest of the U.S. invasion of Cambodia. She then forged a successful business career in technology and was serving on the board of advisors to her College when the formal graduation was finally held.

Tania has climbed Mount Whitney and Mount Kenya, circumnavigated Annapurna, trekked through Bhutan and Kashmir, and sailed along remote rivers in Burma. In 2013 she landed in Nairobi the day of the terrorist attack and proceeded on a walk across that country from beneath Kilimanjaro to the Indian Ocean.

She watched, from afar, the disintegration of the country where her life story began. Those bitter Yugoslav wars of the 1990s put her mother Zora's sisters onto opposing sides of a battle, and not for the first time. Fluent in the languages of her parents, she visits her homelands to study her past. In her book, *Mother Tongue*, she explores, in a highly personal saga, the causes and consequences of Balkan struggles over the last hundred years.

Tania is the author of tales of travel to lands as diverse as Russia, India, Japan and Morocco. She is currently writing a book that starts with her father's flight as an infant from Russia during the Revolution of 1917, follows him through life in Serbia, and to San Francisco's Tsarist Russian community. The essay on her visit to her father's home village in the deep heart of Russia during repressive Communist times was published in *The Best Travel Writing, Volume 10*.

Tania resides in San Francisco, using that city as her base for her worldwide travels.

CPSIA information can be obtained
at www.ICGtesting.com
Printed in the USA
BVHW04*0320300518
517689BV00003B/23/P